Dictatorship for Beginners: A Guide to Taking Over (Almost) Everything

H. M. Tan

Published by Six Scribes Press, 2025.

While every precaution has been taken in the preparation of this book, the publisher assumes no responsibility for errors or omissions, or for damages resulting from the use of the information contained herein.

DICTATORSHIP FOR BEGINNERS: A GUIDE TO TAKING OVER (ALMOST) EVERYTHING

First edition. March 14, 2025.

Copyright © 2025 H. M. Tan.

ISBN: 978-0987106049

Written by H. M. Tan.

Table of Contents

Introduction: Why Dictatorship is the Ultimate Life Hack 1

Chapter 1: The Art of the Takeover – Starting Small (At Home) . 4

Chapter 2: Workplace Domination – From Cubicle to Corporate Tyrant 9

Chapter 3: Social Gatherings – How to Be the Centre of Attention (Always) 15

Chapter 4: Propaganda 101 – Spin the Narrative Like a Pro 21

Chapter 5: Fear and Loyalty – The Dictator's Toolkit 27

Chapter 6: Dress for Success – The Dictator's Fashion Guide 33

Chapter 7: Perfecting Your Evil Laugh 39

Chapter 8: The Cult of Personality – Making Them Worship You 45

Chapter 9: Handling Rebellion – Crushing Dissent with Style ... 52

Chapter 10: Propaganda and Image Control 59

Chapter 11: Eliminating the Opposition – Clearing the Path to Absolute Power 66

Chapter 12: The Dictator's Retirement Plan – Bowing Out with Panache 72

Chapter 13: A Short Compendium of the Very Worst 78

Appendix: Dictator Hall of Fame 117

Author's Note 125

For Steffy, Partner & Dictator

Introduction: Why Dictatorship is the Ultimate Life Hack

Welcome, future Supreme Leader, Benevolent Overlord, or Aspirant to Eternal Power! You've just taken the first step toward trading your mediocre, rules-bound existence for one of pure, unadulterated domination. Here in the world of dictatorship, every red tape, opposing voice, and pesky law bends to your iron will—or conveniently "disappears." If you've always dreamed of having your every whim enforced by a secret police force, congratulations! You've found your calling.

What's so great about dictatorship, you ask? For starters, rules are for the weak, and *you* —my dear tyrant-in-the-making—are not weak. Why settle for polite negotiation when you can command obedience with the wave of a hand (or the threat of exile to a conveniently harsh island)? You'll quickly see the beauty of having *absolute power*: no arguments, no compromises, just smooth sailing on the high seas of despotism. Plus, history has proven again and again that dictators manage to snag all the coolest perks—customised palaces, cult followings, and the magical ability to turn your birthday into a national holiday. And unless you've been trapped inside some Thai cave, know this: *everybody's* doing it: from scammers in third world banana republics to gun-toting militia men in obscure African fiefdoms to capitalist arse-kissers in the good old Uncle Sam!

A Brief History of Ruling Like a Boss

Dictatorship isn't just a modern phenomenon—it's the ultimate old-school power move. Julius Caesar made "crossing the Rubicon" a permanent mood when he decided Rome would be a lot more fun without a Senate constantly nagging. Fast forward to the 20th and 21st centuries, and you've got characters like Stalin, Hitler, Mao, and, yes, everyone's favourite shirtless horseman, Vladimir Putin. What makes dictators so irresistible? It's not just the charisma, absurd monuments, and fabulously inappropriate spending habits. It's their ability to convince millions that they—and *only* they—have the answers to life's greatest questions.

Of course, there's a lot to learn from history's greatest and most infamous dictators. Some ruled through fear, others through absurd levels of control, and a few (we're looking at you, Gaddafi) with off-the-charts eccentricity. Sure, their methods were often horrifying, but you've got to admire the sheer audacity.

Why This Book Exists

Because being nice is overrated, *okay*? Tired of being told "no" in life? Sick of taking orders from bosses, partners, or that smug GPS voice that insists *recalculating* is your only option? Fear not, because this book is here to guide you to the ultimate life hack. Beneath the brutality and war crimes, dictatorship is essentially just living your best life without anyone stopping you. When they go low, you go *lower* baby, right down the tunnel and under them for that almighty ambush.

Sure, you might be wondering, "But isn't dictatorship a bad thing?" History says yes. *This book says no.* Why confine yourself to one lifetime of mediocrity when tyrants have proven again and again that, with the right mix of charisma, paranoia, and violent crackdowns, you can live like a god? You don't have to follow all their footsteps (just skip the genocide parts—bad PR), but the rules of the dictator's game can apply to anyone who dreams big enough.

Exercise Time

Before we go further on this tyrannical adventure, take a moment to grab a pen and some paper—or dictate to your smart assistant if you're already in dictator mode. Write down **three things you'd do if no one**

could say "no" to you. (Be honest, we won't judge... unless it's too tame, in which case we *will* judge.)

1. Would you indiscriminately use the word **woke** to sound important?
2. Trick Kylie into performing at your personal birthday bash?
3. Rename all major landmarks after yourself?

Dream big, because dictators don't do small. If your answers involve a gold-plated yacht, congratulations! You're already thinking like a true autocrat.

And finally, a little humour to kick things off.

> Why did the dictator bring a ladder to the bar?
> To raise the spirits of the people!

Now, brace yourself. The chapters ahead will unlock everything you need to know about crafting your legacy of dominance. Power awaits, my friend. Don't keep it waiting.

Chapter 1: The Art of the Takeover – Starting Small (At Home)

Congratulations, aspiring tyrant! Before you conquer nations, corporations, or even your local homeowner's association, you must first master the ultimate proving ground for dictators-in-training—the household. Yes, where power struggles are as common as unwashed dishes and control of the thermostat is worth more than gold. Dictatorship, like charity, begins at home.

This chapter is your blueprint to becoming the Supreme Leader of your own four walls. By the time we're done here, you'll rule your living room with an iron fist (and a well-cushioned throne), commanding respect, fear, and, if you're lucky, someone else to take the trash out.

How-To: Declare Yourself the Supreme Leader of the Household

The first step to absolute power? A public proclamation. Nothing says "I'm in charge" quite like setting the tone with bombastic declarations. It doesn't matter if your realm consists only of your spouse, children, and the family goldfish—every despot starts small.

Step 1 – Craft Your Title and Vision

Forget boring titles like "Dad" or "Mom." You need something dripping with authority. May we suggest "The Thermostatic Overlord" or "Sovereign Keeper of All Household Snacks"? Your title should simultaneously command respect and confuse anyone attempting rebellion.

From here, outline your vision for your household. Declare that everyone must rise at 6 AM for their national anthem (which you will write, sung to the tune of "Happy Birthday"). Set rules like "all requests for snacks must be submitted in triplicate" or prohibit the touching of the Wi-Fi router without a signed decree. Be firm, be ridiculous, and above all, be specific.

Step 2 – Establish Control of Resources

No dictator rises to power without controlling the resources, and your house is no different. Take ownership of the three most important assets:

1. The TV remote – Whoever holds this dictates the cultural diet of your household. Today, it's your favourite soap opera. Tomorrow, it's *dictator documentaries* on repeat.
2. The Wi-Fi password – Renaming the network to something like "Obey_TheLeader_OrElse" is a fantastic first step. Only loyal subjects are granted access.
3. The air-con remote, *people* – This device is the nuclear football of the suburban dictator. Keep the temperature at your comfort level and remind everyone who holds the power to turn up the heat (it's not them).

Step 3 – Form Your Inner Circle

Recruit loyalists. These are the individuals who will defend your honour against insurgents (aka family members). Typically, your pet makes the perfect ally. Dogs are loyal and already experts in heeling. Offer them cushy titles like "Official Snack Taster" or "Commander of Couch Naps." Kids can also be wooed with titles like "Minister of Ice Cream Logistics" as long as you bribe them heavily. Divide and conquer, buddy.

Step 4 – Declare a State of Emergency

Every dictator's rise to power includes a *crisis*—an excuse to seize unprecedented control. Your state of emergency could be a trivial household problem. A clogged sink? Declare martial law in the kitchen. Missing car keys? Blame the youngest and restrict their access to cartoons as punishment. Chaos is your ally here.

Historical Parallel: Napoleon Bonaparte, the Micromanagement Maestro

Take cues from none other than Napoleon Bonaparte, who, before conquering much of Europe, was incredibly adept at controlling his surroundings. Reports indicate that Napoleon was notoriously hands-on, even dictating the exact way his staff arranged furniture and dressed him each morning. He famously maintained control of every letter written in his name, editing with an obsessive flair.

Following his example, leave no household decision unchecked. Regularly inspect the correct alignment of throw pillows, whether trash cans are emptied to your liking, and how evenly the peanut butter is spread on sandwiches. Micromanagement isn't micromanagement when you're Supreme Leader; it's "quality assurance."

Practical Exercises for Dictators-in-Training

Dictatorship must be polished daily. You're not just seizing power—you're cultivating an aura of unquestionable authority! Here are some exercises to hone your skills:

1. **Practice Your Commanding Stare**
   The stare determines everything. Stand in front of a mirror and channel your inner James Bond villain. Tilt just one eyebrow, smirk faintly, and look as if you know everyone's

Netflix password without asking. Five minutes daily is all it takes to mesmerize peasants (or your unwilling teenager, same thing).

2. **Conduct a Loyalty Test**
Pick a random family member and ask them to fetch something pointless, like a glass of water for your pet cactus. Their obedience without questioning indicates loyalty. If they hesitate, draft a written warning, complete with ominous stamps.

3. **Draw Up a Family Constitution**
If no one else steps forward to write the rules, your word becomes law. Use statements such as, "All sibling disputes shall be settled in front of the Supreme Leader," and "The dishwasher is off-limits without proper certifications." Remember, bureaucracy saps rebellion.

Pro Tip: Rule With Both Fear and Love

History repeatedly proves the most successful dictators skilfully tread the line between earning admiration and scaring the living daylights out of their subjects. Be like the Roman emperor Trajan, who built nearly a cult following with bread and circuses but terrified anyone who dared stand in his way. Master both strategies.

- To foster fear, use guilt trips and vague threats. Phrases like, "I would hate for someone to lose remote privileges," or "It would be a shame if chores doubled tomorrow..." work like magic.
- To secure love, deploy small rewards—TV privileges, chore exemptions, or insider knowledge of your secret candy stash. These crumbs of kindness will tie their loyalty to you like Velcro.

Pro Tip Bonus Exercise

For seasoned dictators-in-training, take it up a notch by instituting a "Daylight Savings Bank." Convince household members that they must earn hours of daylight by completing tasks you assign. Redeemable daylight hours are, of course, entirely fictional—but what follower will question brilliance?

> Why did the dictator's dog never bury bones in the backyard?
> Because it only followed *orders*, not instincts.

Dealing With Disobedience and Resistance

Inevitably, someone will get the bright idea to resist your iron-fisted rule. Perhaps it's your spouse suggesting that they, too, want input on the dinner menu (*the audacity*). Or maybe your teenager decides "Supreme Snack Overlord" is no longer a valid authority.

Here's the trick—reframe rebellion as treasonous selfishness. Casually drop the phrase, "This wouldn't happen under North Korean discipline," during conversations. Remind them that the last victim of rebellion ended up folding three weeks' worth of laundry as punishment.

When all else fails, institute exile. Send defiant subjects to the freezing basement with no blanket or, worse, to the nearest dull family reunion as your stand-in.

Real-Life Example

Kim Jong-un—a dictator closer to our own time—famously gathered unrelenting loyalty through extravagant family dinners where attendees had no choice but to raise several toasts honouring him. Picture this at your dinner table. Command everyone to toast "The One Who Magnanimously Allows (insert the treat of the day here)".

Chapter 2: Workplace Domination – From Cubicle to Corporate Tyrant

Ah, the workplace. A realm of fluorescent lights, temperamental coffee machines, and passive-aggressive sticky notes. For an aspiring tyrant like you, it's not just a dreary 9-to-5—it's fertile ground for empire-building. After all, every corporate czar—from Steve Jobs to Kenny "The Spreadsheet Slayer" in Accounting—had to start somewhere. This chapter will teach you how to rise from a lowly cubicle dweller to an unopposed corporate overlord. Your coworkers won't know what hit them.

The key is simple: disrupt, dominate, and dazzle. Sure, the HR policy manual might frown upon world domination in the workplace, but policies are for other people. You've got mountains of office supplies to conquer and breakroom allegiances to forge.

How-To: Hijacking the Workplace with Style

When you walk into the office, it's not enough to exist—you must grip your domain by the stapler and declare it yours. Lucky for you, the workplace is full of ripe opportunities for control, manipulation, and, dare we say, creative dictatorship.

Step 1 – Cultivate Your Aura of Authority

First things first, appearances matter. A true corporate dictator doesn't blend into the sea of business casual drones. They stand out. Here's how to curate an air of gravitas that makes people think twice about interrupting your coffee break.

- **Wardrobe:** Drop the khakis. Think power. Sharp suits, stylish blazers, or even a signature accessory that doubles as a symbol of your reign—say, a cape. Nothing says "I run this

place" like leather gloves or a monocle at an all-hands meeting.
- **Posture:** Stand tall. Always look like you're on the verge of reinventing the wheel or firing half the company (even if you're just daydreaming about dim sims).
- **Vocal Tone:** Speak with the conviction of someone whose lunch NEVER gets stolen from the fridge. Slow, deliberate, and laced with just a hint of menace.

Step 2 – Seize the High Ground (Literally and Figuratively)

Position yourself as the centrepiece of operations, even if you're technically miles below middle management. Start with small victories like hijacking meetings. Sit at the head of the table without asking. Begin taking notes aloud, inserting phrases like, "We should circle back to this once I have final approval." People will soon forget you weren't invited in the first place.

One pro-level tactic involves controlling endless office memos. Adopt the mantra, "I'll cc who I want." From there, flood inboxes with suggestions and sly power grabs like, "Shall we restructure the committee to align with my vision?" or "I've gone ahead and taken the liberty of leading this initiative."

Watch as the sheep nod along helplessly.

Step 3 – Establish Ownership Over Shared Resources

You cannot rule an office without securing coveted communal assets. Focus on these key battlegrounds for total workplace takeover.

1. **The Coffee Machine**
   Change the settings, "suggest upgrades," or guard the supply of premium beans as if it's a national treasure. Bonus points if you distribute inferior coffee to the masses while sipping your

personal, artisanal blend from a dictator-worthy mug.
2. **The Office Playlist**
Declare dominion over any shared speakers. Curating music may seem noble, but it's strategic. Blast classical imperial marches or obscure ambient techno to keep morale confusingly low yet focused.
3. **The Conference Room Schedule**
Book recurring "strategy meetings," which consist exclusively of you swivelling in the chair and dictating your conquests. Name your private sessions something cryptic like "Operation Phoenix" to stoke curiosity and fear.
4. **Snacks**
Start with subtle changes—claim peanut butter rights or require "Snackfest Proposals." Soon, all almonds pass through you. Congratulations, you are now the Corporate Sultan of Salted Cashews.

Step 4 – Create a Cult of Personality

Steve Jobs practically trademarked this concept. Infamously described as having a "reality distortion field," he convinced employees that the impossible was achievable purely because he demanded it.

You can achieve similar results. Start by making every victory, no matter how minor, sound like a groundbreaking triumph. Persuade others that your creative flair is a rare intellectual blessing ("A triple-ply toilet paper suggestion? I reinvented the breakroom!"). Refer to your workspace as "The Command Centre," and never downplay your genius, even when stapling papers.

Build loyal followers. Begin by targeting those on the lower end of office hierarchy. Praise their menial contributions as acts of unparalleled brilliance. For example, "Jessica, that photocopying job inspired this month's workflow overhaul." They'll follow you forever.

Step 5 – Redefine Team Projects

Here's the thing about dictators—they rarely build anything themselves. That's what minions are for. But the illusion of collaboration is indispensable. Always be "leading" team efforts while subtly claiming the lion's share of credit.

When a project succeeds, ensure your name appears in bold at the top of every slide deck. When it fails (don't pretend this won't happen), redirect blame faster than a CEO avoiding shareholders. "Mark insisted we follow his outdated spreadsheet model" should work.

The Relatable Tyrant™ – Striking Fear and Building Trust Simultaneously

True office dictatorship isn't just about ruling with intimidation. It's about balancing fear and love, as every great dictator does. Be actively unpredictable—pleasant one moment, thunderous the next— to keep coworkers perpetually uneasy. For inspiration, recall the infamous workplace leaders like Jeff Bezos, whose fiery outbursts are matched only by his team's reverential loyalty.

Fear Tactics

Subtlety wins here. Suggest consequences without being explicit, like, "This report better shine like gold, or else…" The "or else" is best left ambiguous. Smile after delivering your message. Psychologically, no one will underestimate a tyrant with dimples.

Trust Tactics

Throw the occasional "office camaraderie moment." Organise takeout lunches but ensure you're at the head of the table. Invite workers to join your elite inner circle ("The Productivity Council") for special recognition—then ostracise them when they underperform.

Historical Inspiration – Stalin in the Workplace

While Joseph Stalin didn't grace us with PowerPoint, his workplace operations were legendary. His infamous purges turned "snitches" into relics of the past, and his ability to rewrite inconvenient truths set the gold standard for shady memo editing. Of course, we recommend softer versions of his methods—like conveniently deleting a coworker from cc threads when they step out of line.

Pro Tips for Dominators-in-the-Making

- **Office Scapegoating 101** – Identify a coworker who routinely "complicates" tasks you pass off. Mention their name each time something falls apart. It's subtle but effective.
- **Confuse and Conquer** – Adopt corporate jargon no one understands. Phrases like "synergising visibility toward deliverables" are excellent for appearing revolutionary while sowing confusion.

Exercises

1. **Draft Your First Workplace Executive Order:**
   Examples include, "Casual Friday now requires formal tilts of the hat," or "All snack wrappers must be surrendered for inspection." Publish on the fridge for maximum impact.
2. **Perfect Your Pensive Gaze on Zoom:**
   During virtual meetings, frequently stroke your chin or nod sagely with furrowed brows. Screenshot yourself mid-session to evaluate your aura of seriousness.

Why did the dictator bring a pencil to the boardroom?
To draw the line on collaboration.

How to Crush Resistance

Eventually, your coworkers will have questions like, "Who died and made *you* boss?" These are rebranded rebellions and must be handled swiftly. Powerful rebuttals include:

- "If you want democracy, may I suggest a grade school playground?"
- "I'm merely optimising chaos for greater efficiency."

Finally, always have an escape plan. When the uprising grows, retreat to HR with a strategic grievance. Blame everything on brewing "toxicity" among your subordinates, complete with spreadsheets for theatrical flair.

Why did the office dictator throw their chair out the window?
To make sure the next meeting had "standing room only."

By mastering these steps, you'll transform from timid worker bee to full-blown corporate tyrant. Remember—the office isn't just where you work. It's where you reign.

Chapter 3: Social Gatherings – How to Be the Centre of Attention (Always)

Congratulations, oh aspiring ruler of revelry! Conquering the art of social domination is your next step toward immortal greatness—or at least securing the last slice of pizza at a BBQ. Social gatherings are perfect training grounds for your budding dictatorship, as they're microcosms of society filled with awkward small talk and unattended snack tables. Parties, after all, aren't just about fun—they're about power.

The key to standing out and bending social events to your will is simple: make everything about you. From commandeering the conversational spotlight to restructuring party rules in your favour, this chapter will arm you with everything you need to monopolise attention and ensure no one leaves without knowing you were *the* main character of the evening.

How-To: Become the Dictator of Any Social Event

Just like kings of old didn't waltz across battlefields without a plan, you can't saunter into a party expecting to dominate on charisma alone (though it helps). It takes strategy, flair, and the willingness to ban Monopoly during game night because *"only your version of Risk captures the true spirit of competition."*

Step 1 – Declare Your Rule as "The Fun Dictator"

Any social dictator worth their champagne coup knows that a self-proclaimed title paves the way to dominance. Referring to yourself as "The Party President" or "Chairman of Charcuterie" might seem ridiculous, but it projects confidence. After all, dictators never second-guess themselves—and neither should you.

Use your title to create a narrative. Say it aloud when you enter. "The Fun Dictator has arrived!" Drop casual comments like, "Remember, it's my job to keep this party alive," whenever anyone seems to be having less fun than required. Soon, your reign will feel as natural to others as their fear of karaoke.

Step 2 – Corner the Conversation Sphere

A dictator doesn't wait for attention—they seize it. Your conversational strategy needs to combine charm and sheer, relentless persistence.

- **Monopolize with anecdotes:** Ensure your stories are longer, louder, and (preferably) only tangentially related to the topics at hand. Did someone mention skiing? Launch into a five-minute saga about how you "single-handedly tamed Switzerland's most dangerous slopes" (even if by slopes you meant the hotel bar).
- **Interrupt strategically:** The weak wait their turn to speak, but not you. Timing is crucial. Interrupt when another guest reaches the peak of their joke—bonus points if you follow up with a louder and "funnier" punchline that has nothing to do with theirs.
- **Pose as the guru:** Socializing is about hierarchy, so establish yourself as the all-knowing sage. Correct trivial facts like drink recipes or the number of countries in Europe, even if you have no earthly clue. Your confidence is what sells it, not accuracy.

Step 3 – Control the Activities

To rule a social gathering, it's essential to weaponize your natural dictator instinct for restructuring systems. Every game or discussion is an opportunity to assert dominance—or, as you'll call it, "improve the fun for everyone."

- **Ban Boring Games:** Prohibit anything involving luck or chance; skill-based games give you a clear advantage. Invent overly complicated rules designed for your victory. Replace "Kickball" with "Supreme Leader Ball," adding obscure penalties like "you can't run unless humming the national anthem I just made up." People will comply out of sheer bewilderment.
- **Curate the Playlist:** Your music taste is the social lubricant everyone needs. Replace all background songs with what you deem appropriate—upbeat tunes during your speeches, orchestral pieces during your food selection moments, and dramatic drum rolls as you unveil the fruit platter.
- **Theming Is Key:** Can every gathering be turned into a dictatorship-themed soirée? Yes. Mandate costumes like "revolutionary chic" or "generalissimo lounge wear." Anyone who shows up underdressed can be "exiled" to the backyard.

Step 4 – Foster Dependence on Your Entertainment Monopoly

Human beings crave fun, and like all good rulers, you must manipulate that dependency. Subtly position yourself as the one who *makes* the evening interesting.

- Begin every event with obscure trivia only you know (completely fabricated trivia is fine). "Did you know the average person eats four live spiders at BBQs? Better hope that grilled sausage is clean!"
- Master the art of surprise to keep guests on edge. Suddenly declare, "TIME FOR THE ICEBREAKER QUESTION

ROUND!" mid-conversation. No one will oppose because they won't have time to think.

Real-Life Parallels – Kim Jong-un's Legendary Parties

Legend has it that North Korea's supreme leader, Kim Jong-un, knows a thing or two about unforgettable parties. Attendance? Mandatory. Entertainment? Extravagant. Reputation? One of someone who dictates the tone of life itself.

Adopt his approach at your next gathering. Create an air of exclusivity— "Only *my* parties have an actual toastmaster!" Make your mere presence feel like a privilege. Like Kim, ensure every mention of your soirées becomes pre-emptively awe-inspiring. Soon, people will RSVP "yes" out of a mixture of dread and curiosity—precisely what we're aiming for.

Pro Tip – Bring an Entourage to Laugh at Your Jokes

A dictator is only as funny as their audience makes them appear. Surround yourself with an entourage—a handpicked cadre of loyal followers who laugh on cue during your best (and worst) moments. Strategic placements (by the snack table, conversational bottlenecks) ensure laughter reaches all corners of the room.

Nothing amplifies a social ruler's charisma like a few well-timed guffaws. Bonus points for bribing someone to yell, "You're so smart!" after every trivia question.

Practical Exercises for Social Tyrants

1. **Interrupt Mid-Sentence Practice:**
   Interrupting people with grace is an art. Start small. At home, jump in over boring dinner conversations. Build confidence

until you can silence an entire room.
2. **Invent a New Rule "On the Fly":**
At your next gathering, announce a food-related rule no one expects. For example, "No one can refill their plate without reciting their favourite trait about me!" Watch compliance skyrocket out of confusion.

> Why did the dictator ban whipped cream at the party?
> Because he only tolerates *unwhipped* people!

Handling Party Rebels

Of course, there will always be naysayers—attention-seekers trying to steal your spotlight by telling better jokes or overthrowing your playlist authority (sacrilege!). They must be neutralised promptly but efficiently.

- **Pre-emptively Dismiss Challenges:** Wave off their quips with a line like, "That's great, Ted, but some of us were born with *actual* charisma."
- **Invoke Ridicule:** Transform dissent into a running gag everyone can laugh at— "Remember last time Jim tried to bring his playlist? It was ALL Nickelback!"

Advanced Social Manipulation Moves

Feeling ambitious? Graduate into truly Machiavellian techniques by reshaping the social landscape subtly but completely.

- Announce favoured guests ("top-tier invitees") to sow envy.
- Nominate yourself as the "Evening's Arbiter," delivering objective (or not-so-objective) rulings on every disagreement.

> Why did the dictator annex the punch bowl?
> To ensure he *stirred* the people's spirits!

The Aftermath – Cementing Your Legacy

The moment the final song plays and guests reluctantly leave, your work isn't done. The true mark of social dictatorship is ensuring every event becomes *legendary*. Use group chats to repost highlight moments, proclaim your party theme as "award-winning," and casually suggest it's *the* standard for future gatherings.

Eventually, your reign over barbecues, book clubs, and birthdays will solidify, leaving no doubt that you're the supreme leader of good times.

Remember, social gatherings aren't just about having fun—they're about ensuring you're the one people have fun *because* of. Now go claim your social kingdom!

Chapter 4: Propaganda 101 – Spin the Narrative Like a Pro

Welcome, dear despot-in-the-making, to the hallowed halls of narrative manipulation! If conquest is the heart of dictatorship, propaganda is its blood—circulating your truth, your glory, and *only* your version of events to the masses (or, in more relatable terms, your social circle, workplace, or Twitter followers). A kingdom isn't built on facts; it's built on the cleverly spun story that elevates you to godlike status.

This chapter is your crash course in propaganda artistry. From rewriting family arguments in your favour to causing actual history books to declare you Supreme Overachiever of the Century, you'll soon wield storytelling like an imperial sceptre.

How-To: Control the Story, Control the People

Spin doctors don't rely on objective truths. They create narratives that hypnotize, confuse, or simply bore the crowd into submission. To wield this level of mind control, you'll need to think bigger than fake news. You're reshaping reality itself!

Step 1 – Build Your Brand and Stick to It

Every great dictator has a brand. Stalin was the stoic father figure. Mussolini thought he was the human embodiment of charisma (spoiler alert: he wasn't). Napoleon? Napoleonic intensity in every short step he took.

Your brand is crucial to maintaining narrative dominance. Are you the visionary leader unfairly undervalued by mere mortals? The tireless saviour protecting your people from their oh-so-wicked neighbours (or coworkers)? Pick one and promote it tirelessly.

Never allow inconsistencies. If you're "The Worker's Ally," for instance, you can't be caught lounging in first-class with champagne. Spin it! Claim, "I'm only here to observe how the elite mistreat service staff for *research purposes*." The truth is irrelevant; the story is sacrosanct.

Step 2 – Social Media Domination

Raise your hand if you've had an unflattering photo haunt you for years. Now imagine if someone scrolled past that photo daily, deciding whether you deserved to wield power. Nightmare, right? That's why dictators *dominate* social media, ensuring that every upload screams strength, style, and fluoride-enriched teeth.

- **The Heroic Feed**
  Your Instagram profile must become a shrine commemorating your greatness. Post pictures of you pretending to read difficult-looking books (bonus points if it's upside-down). Make sure every Facebook status paints you as relatable but untouchably brilliant. For example, "Just reminded my team today that even greatness takes coffee. #HumbleLeaderStuff."
- **Strategic Hashtags**
  Extend your influence on every corner of the internet using hashtags like #RelatablePower, #LeaderEnergy, and #TheyWillThankMeLater. Ambiguity is key! A vague post with a gorgeous pic will have people filling in the blanks with their admiration.
- **Takedown Opposition**
  Is someone daring to call out your propaganda skills? Too much honesty in your Twitter replies? Easy fix. Gaslight

them by replying, "Funny you think that... *but did you actually read the policy I put forward?*" Follow up with a 4,000-character thread no one will read.

Step 3 – Invent Enemies. Blame Liberally.

Propaganda Rule #1 (which you should tattoo on your forehead in invisible ink): Nothing unites like fear of a shared enemy. True or false doesn't matter; what matters is their utility. The "enemy" could be vague buzzwords like "disloyalty" or hilariously specific scapegoats like the neighbour who *definitely* sabotaged your garden.

Real-life dictators perfected this. Joseph Goebbels, the morally bankrupt mastermind of Nazi propaganda, invented bogeymen to justify every wrongheaded policy. (Of course, his enemies were entirely evil constructs—we, on the other hand, will focus on benign garden-variety control tactics. We have *class*.)

Here's what you can do in your sphere of influence:

- Paint yourself as the people's shield. "If it weren't for me," you'll say gravely, "we'd all be succumbing to Jeff's lame PowerPoints about synergy."
- Any inconvenience? Redirect the blame to your fabricated foe. Did the holiday party run out of appetisers? Say, "It's exactly what happened when people trusted Sharon from HR last time."

Step 4 – The Art of the Distraction

When rumours about your double-crosses (or unpaid parking tickets) start swirling, you must learn to wield distractions like a Jedi wields a lightsabre. People can't focus on your misdeeds if you're constantly throwing shiny objects into their gaze.

A few classic tactics include:

- **The Flashy Announcement**
  Did you neglect to finish your presentation but still claim you'd revolutionize office workflows? Redirect failure attention by saying, "We're launching a Break Room Cookie Restocking Initiative." Boldness is the distraction; bickies are collateral.
- **The Scandalous Decoy**
  Plant rumours so juicy no one will care about your actual nonsense. For example, float the idea that Brenda in IT is secretly living off-grid, returning only to upload memes.

Step 5 – Repeat Lies Until They Become Truths

The key to a successful lie isn't cleverness—it's repetition. Repeat yourself so often and confidently that even *you* begin to believe your wildest nonsense. Twice impeached U.S. President Donald J Trump does this *all the time*! Joseph Goebbels famously said, "A lie told once remains a lie, but a lie told a thousand times becomes the truth." (Do not Google him for other ideas. Seriously—don't.)

Want to erase certain family "incidents?" Insist that *your* version of the argument (where you graciously forgave Aunt Edna for *her* issues, not yours) is the universal truth until every holiday greeting starts with "Thank you for being the bigger person last year."

Real-Life Parallel – The North Korean Kim Dynasty

You've got to hand it to the Kims—they've practically monopolized the concept of self-mythologizing through propaganda. Kim Jong-un reportedly invented miraculous legends about himself before the age of 10. Need proof? North Korean textbooks claim, among other things, that he was a pro driver as a toddler.

No one can back this up, but no one dares dispute it either. That, my dear tyrant, is the *essence* of impeccable propaganda.

Pro Tips for a Masterclass in Spinning the Narrative

- **The Apology Duck-and-Dodge:**
  When cornered, stage a highly theatrical apology filled with generic phrases like, "We *must* learn from this misstep." Finish with, "Moving forward under my guidance will prevent such unfortunate errors." Boom—you're both contrite and indispensable.
- **Visual Propaganda Wins the Day:**
  Photos of you holding adorable puppies or personally handing out food (even if it's staged) are worth gold. Add blur filters for extra drama.
- **Gaslighting 201:**
  Advanced use of gaslighting involves making people think they're lucky to be misinformed. "Lucky for you, I handle the tough stuff. You don't need to know the details!"

Practical Exercises

1. **Spin Your Resume:** Rewrite your CV so it reads like a heroic saga instead of a job history. "Soft Skills" becomes "Legendary Peacemaker in Friday Status Meetings." "Excel Knowledge" becomes "Tyrant of Data."
2. **Rebrand a Failure:** Pick a recent loss (like burning dinner) and frame it differently. Example? "I'm proving the resilience of smoke alarms. This event was an engineered safety test."

Why did the dictator start posting selfies?
To control both the narrative *and* the angles.

Crush Opposition Quicker Than a Censor Bell

Sometimes, crafty rebels (read as "annoying relatives or coworkers") may attempt fact-checking. How dare they! Here's how to squash dissent in artisanally petty ways:

- Reply to their questions with irrelevant counter-questions.
- Label critics as "uninformed" and offer a fictional bibliography.
- Quietly edit any challenging proof in their emails to show they supported *you* all along.

Why did the propagandist buy a thesaurus?
To make lies sound *extra true*!

Retrofitting Your Greatness into History

The final touch of any propaganda campaign is rewriting history itself to amplify your contributions (and conveniently erase your flaws). Create timelines where your name appears under pivotal events like "2015–2023 Spread Peace (and Killer Tweets)" and prominently display photos of yourself shaking hands with people, regardless of context.

Remember, the only thing louder than a dictator's voice is their legend—and you're about to go viral for all the right reasons.

With propaganda in your toolkit, you no longer react to events. Instead, you *define* what happened, why, and how glorious you were while doing it. Now go forth with dramatic Instagram captions and spin reality like the unapologetic artist you are!

Chapter 5: Fear and Loyalty – The Dictator's Toolkit

Welcome back, dear aspiring overlord! Thus far, you've mastered the art of seizing control, dazzling the masses, and spinning reality to suit your narrative. But power is a fickle beast, and to keep it leashed, you'll need an iron grip—and maybe some emotional puppy eyes. This is where the dictator's best tools come into play: *fear* and *loyalty*.

Think of these two forces as your Yin and Yang. Too much fear, and your underlings might turn on you (pitchforks are never flattering). Too much loyalty without discipline, and you'll end up with a team of saps doodling hearts around your name. The trick is balance. You want enough fear to keep people in awe (or mildly terrified) and enough loyalty to guarantee three rounds of applause when you so much as sneeze.

How-To: Command Fear Without Becoming a Cartoon Villain

Fear isn't just about screaming orders or brandishing metaphorical whips. (Unless you're at an improv night—it's a niche audience.) True mastery of fear involves psychological finesse. You want people to both respect and dread you, questioning every little action, as if disobedience might result in a "mandatory discussion."

Step 1 – The Artful Threat

The best threats aren't explicit; they're implied. Stalin was a master of this game. The man would smile at you over a vodka toast while subtly suggesting that being late on your next report could result in your family's sudden "relocation." Dark? Yes. Effective? 100%.

For a softer 21st-century take:

- **The Slow Smile:** Perfect your unsettling smile. When someone underperforms, don't berate them; just look, pause, and smile like you're already plotting something. The key is to leave them wondering.
- **Ambiguous Warnings:** "I'd hate for anything... unexpected to happen during our team presentation." "I trust you'll follow through; you wouldn't want to disappoint me *again*." The vaguer, the better.

Step 2 – Public Spectacles (Without Total Chaos)

Fear works best when others witness you holding someone accountable. This ensures the entire group knows rebellion equals consequences (and potentially zero birthday cakes at office parties).

Suggestions for modern fear-mongering antics include:

- Subtly ousting someone from a group project for insufficient "team spirit."
- Withholding snacks or coveted privileges from those who dare question you. Covet the box of donuts out loud, saying, "Only those with excellent attendance deserve frosting."
- Lovingly adopt a public diss strategy, e.g., "You tried your best, Mark. Unfortunately, your best is mediocre at our level."

Step 3 – Ride the Unpredictability Train

Imagine going a week without being predictable. Sometimes you're warm and gracious; other times, you're delivering feedback like Gordon Ramsay on a bad soufflé day. You want your people perpetually unsure of which version of you they'll encounter, keeping everyone *just anxious enough*.

Kim Jong-un, for instance, reportedly rewards loyalty one day with a luxury spread and punishes perceived slights the next with a silent, terrifying stare. (Optional side note for those who own cats—observe how felines alternate between affection and mystery.)

Practical application for unpredictability:

- Call team meetings just to decide trivial things like how much ice should be in the office water cooler. Then cancel the meeting abruptly. "Never mind, I've made the executive decision myself."
- Reward a loyal follower with a gift (say, a coffee on you), but heavily imply it's only because they've been "just good enough to deserve it."

How-To: Earn Loyalty Without Losing Your Edge

Fear alone won't inspire the masses to follow you down the proverbial rabbit hole. Loyalty is what convinces people to keep marching even when all signs suggest they should turn back. But earning loyalty takes effort, strategy, and—you guessed it—*a sprinkle of manipulation*.

Step 1 – The Benevolent Dictator Act

Every once in a while, perform an act so generous it borders on saintly, and your loyalists will forever sing your praises (or at least remember to refill your coffee the next time they're at Starbucks). A gift here, a listening ear there, a heartfelt "How are you doing? (No really, it's fine if you cry!)"—these small gestures foster a cultish sense of admiration.

For example:

- Host an elaborate lunch where you call out the "Employee of the Month" (even if it's obviously you).
- Publicly forgive a minor faux pas but whisper something mysterious like, "Just don't make a habit of it."

Stalin himself distributed accolades sparingly, calling loyal subjects "heroes of the state" when it suited him. Pro-tip? Trophies work even better when they're imaginary, like naming someone "Controller of the Remote."

Step 2 – Sowing Seeds of Privilege

No one feels more special than someone who's elevated above their peers. Play favourites but do it transparently enough that people scramble to become your new "favourite." (Congratulations! You've just created an economy of obsequious behaviour.)

Ways to boost loyalty through privilege:

- Distribute arbitrary yet memorable titles like "Vice President of Pie Allocation" or "Grand Marshal of the Coffee Break." These mean nothing, but recipients will defend their honour until the bitter end.
- Give selective access to "private" privileges, like letting certain people see inside your snack drawer. Even a glimpse is power.

Step 3 – The Public Praise Gambit

Praise people loudly, strategically, and for highly specific acts of obedience. This makes your praise seem meaningful, while simultaneously making everyone else *yearn* to be noticed.

For example:

- "Jessica, fantastic stapling on that handout! Such fire. Such innovation!"
- "Doug, brilliant choice of printer margins. You're a visionary!"

The bonus effect? Others start to emulate Jessica and Doug, hoping to bask in your golden glow.

Real-Life Inspiration – Stalin's Balancing Act

Joseph Stalin was many things, but one of his greatest legacies (aside from his haircut) was his ability to juggle fear and loyalty. No one trusted him, yet they would've jumped into a frozen lake if he snapped his fingers. Why? Because Joseph knew when to weed out disloyalty and when to reward loyalty—albeit rewards that were mostly posthumous.

Obviously, we're shooting for less lethal methods here. Unless Sharon in HR *really* forgets your birthday next year.

Exercises for the Fear-Loyalty Dynamic Mastery

1. **Practice Your Commanding Stares**
   Sit in front of a mirror and experiment with stares tailored to specific emotions. The "Regret Everything Right Now" glare versus the "You Should Feel Grateful I'm This Chill" smirk. Bonus points for sustained eye contact without blinking.
2. **Scapegoat Simulation**
   Identify one minor mishap within your world (e.g., a poorly chosen picnic spot) and scapegoat a neutral party. Test small phrases like, "Well, Jane did suggest it..." to see how far you can subtly shift blame.

Why did the dictator reward the dog? To ensure he'd fetch loyalty, not dissent!

Pro Tips for Perfect Tyrannical Balance

- Always maintain plausible deniability when you're ruling with fear. "Who, me? Scary? What a dramatic statement!"
- Alternate between fear and loyalty-building behaviours like a conductor orchestrating highs and lows in symphonies.
- Reward unexpected devotion publicly but punish rebellion

privately. Fear motivations are camera shy; loyalty thrives in the limelight.

Final Thought – Fear AND Loyalty

Like a perfectly brewed cocktail, the right balance of fear and loyalty leaves people both entranced by and terrified of you. Keep them craving your approval but terrified of earning your wrath—*even a minor* version of your wrath, like scheduling meetings on Fridays at 4 p.m.

When executed with finesse, mastery of fear and loyalty will allow you to dominate every room you enter for years to come. Plus, eight out of ten advisors agree it's *way* better than being nice.

Chapter 6: Dress for Success – The Dictator's Fashion Guide

Ah, fashion—a dictator's not-so-secret weapon. Because what's the point of ruling over the masses if you're not doing it draped in fabrics so immaculate they form their own fan club? A signature look can define your reign, intimidate your rivals, and inspire a generation of costume parties at worst. And like every other dictator-worthy endeavour, your wardrobe must scream, "I'm here to rule, not to blend in with the plebs."

For centuries, leaders have used clothes to say what words cannot (or should not), from Louis XIV and the excess of his golden robes to Muammar Gaddafi and his... eclectic (and often incomprehensible) ensembles. Crafting a dictator's wardrobe is both an art and a science, and by the end of this guide, you'll be ready to dress like your calendar includes invading lunchrooms and overthrowing bake sales.

The Psychology of a Power Outfit

Before you step into your snakeskin boots or military-inspired pantsuit, understand this fundamental truth: your clothing is the first weapon in your arsenal. Fabric isn't just fabric—it's a signal of dominance. A crisp suit says, "I control economies," while an embroidered cape screams, "Bow before me, mortals." Always remember, you're not just dressing for yourself; you're dressing to influence everyone within a 15-km radius.

How-To Fashion Your Way to Supreme Ruler Status

Throw away garments that whisper "normal." You want your closet to look like each item was sewn by blindfolded artists and blessed by ancient prophecies. Here's your step-by-step guide to becoming a style dictator:

Step 1 – Claim a Signature Item

Every legendary leader has their sartorial calling card. Napoleon had his bicorne hat tilted just right; Chairman Mao had his minimalist "Mao suit"; and Gaddafi, well, had *everything plus the kitchen sink*. You, dear dictator-in-the-making, need your own iconography.

- **Caps and Hats:** Nothing says "unstoppable power" like a well-chosen hat. Try a beret. Not ordinary, pedestrian berets, though—think gold-thread embroidery, gemstone accents, and maybe subtle LED lighting. Tilt it at an angle that suggests you *just don't care* about gravity anymore.
- **Monogrammed Capes:** Change every bad day into an epic photo-op with a cape that catches the wind perfectly (or hire a lackey to fan it behind you at all times). Bonus points for fur accents to make animal-rights activists faint.
- **Eyewear of Mystery:** Sunglasses? Mandatory. Oversized and tinted, they say, "You don't need to see into my soul; you wouldn't survive what's in there." Kim Jong-Il reportedly owned pairs so outrageously large, even Elton John applauded.
- **The Military Touch:** Epaulettes are non-negotiable. Are you commanding military forces? No, but your oversized golden shoulder pads don't need that justification. They're there because you're *important*.

Step 2 – Choose Fabrics that Scream Power

Fabric matters—because the wrong polyester blend can ruin even the most dictatorial of intentions. Here's your cheat sheet for dictator-approved materials:

- **Silk and Satin:** Soft enough to snuggle with yet arrogant enough to remind everyone they'll never afford it.
- **Leather—But in Moderation:** Remember, you're a dictator, not a rock band's washed-up bassist. A solid leather jacket or gloves in your wardrobe will add a dose of "don't test me" to any event.
- **Brocade and Velvet:** Regal opulence straight out of Shakespearean drama. Add a feather or two but resist the temptation to literally look like a chesterfield sofa.
- **Gold, Gold, and More Gold:** Glistening metallic threads were practically invented for dictators (and disco). Even your pyjamas should shine brighter than the average person's wedding outfit.

Step 3 – Colour Coordinate for Authority

Colours have meanings—sartorial Greek chorus commentary for your ambitions. Select these dictator-friendly hues to convey power, danger, or sheer magnificence.

- **Black:** Timeless, menacing, and perfect for a power silhouette. Think Darth Vader, but with better tailors.
- **Red:** The universal colour for "Watch out, I'm either in command or about to yell." If Stalin's posters taught us one thing, it's that red shrouds you in revolutionary credibility. Also complements bloodthirst nicely.
- **White:** Risky but rewarding. Wear this when you want to look untouchable, like the incarnation of divine knowledge wrapped in pristine laundry.
- **Gold:** Is gold technically a colour anymore or just a lifestyle choice? Either way, the answer is "yes."

Avoid pastel shades at all costs. You're not a bloody birthday cake hun, so try not to dress like one.

Step 4 – Accessories Make the Tyrant

What good is a power suit without accoutrements that double as conversation starters? Accessories are dictator cherry-on-top moments where you say, "Oh, these diamonds? They're just my weekday rubies."

- **Statement Belts:** No plain leather—the buckle alone should be capable of doubling as dinnerware.
- **Walking Sticks or Ruling Sceptres:** There's something inherently commanding about carrying a stick that doesn't serve any practical purpose. It says, "I walk because I choose to, not because I have to."
- **Limited-Edition Footwear:** Custom boots are essential. The idea isn't just to walk tall—it's to intimidate everyone within kicking distance.
- **Gaudy Jewellery:** Less is not more here. Drape yourself in accessories so clunky that they echo when you move.

Step 5 – The Uniform Effect

Want to assert authority with zero effort? Create a uniform. Dictators love uniforms for the same reason toddlers love capes—it's costumed proof that you're in charge. Customize yours to include medals, ribbons, and unnecessary pockets. If you don't command an army, simply invent one called "The Supreme Style Vanguard."

Real-Life Fashion Dictators – Lessons from the Legends

- **Muammar Gaddafi:** The original "I do what I want" fashion influencer. Gaddafi's wardrobe was a one-man Broadway

spectacle, blending tribal robes, suits dripping in military flair, and outfits made exclusively out of silk and audacity. Iconic moments include wearing aviators indoors and looking like the world's most fashionable Bond villain.
- **Hugo Chávez:** Master of subtle branding, Chávez claimed bold red as his colour, ensuring crowds were painted in his image. He also loved berets, giving him an air of constant, casual coups.
- **Imelda Marcos:** Proof that dictatorship doesn't have to exclude heels; she famously owned more shoes than most people will see in their lifetime.

Exercises for Aspiring Style Tyrants

1. **Choose Your Dictator Colour:** Spend an entire week wearing only one colour. Observe how changing moods—or ridicule—shape your confidence.
2. **Practice the Flare Walk:** Don't just enter a room—*arrive*. Stand in front of a fan (or simulate windy conditions) to perfect your dramatic, cape-enhanced entrance.

Pro Tips for Your Fashion Domination

- When in doubt, overdress. If your outfit feels even slightly appropriate for the occasion, it's too tame.
- Maintain a mystery closet. Nobody should predict what you'll wear next, though everyone should assume it'll blow their minds.
- Build a costume Instagram. Caption every upload with things like, "Someday, kids from Townville to Tokyo will wear this to rebel."

Fashion Dictation as a Legacy

Remember, your personal style won't just be immortalised while you're in charge; it's going to occupy history books, statues, and ironic Halloween costumes for centuries. Dress not for the job you have, but for the jobs of every monarch, conqueror, and action figure that will follow your example.

When you look the part of a ruler, the world kneels a little faster. Go forth, self-declared fashion deity, and strut your way to dominion in 12-inch boots and wind-perfecting capes. Because your rule isn't just a state of mind—it's a state of style.

> How does a dictator organize his closet?
> By executive order.

Chapter 7: Perfecting Your Evil Laugh

Congratulations, future overlord! You've mastered the art of workplace domination, social theatrics, and even dressing like the human embodiment of "don't mess with me." But what happens when all eyes are on you, and words alone won't cut it? Enter the pièce de résistance of the dictator toolkit—*the evil laugh.*

An evil laugh is more than just a sound. It's a power move, a battle cry, and a not-so-subtle reminder to the peasants that yes, you *do* spend your free time plotting their eventual submission. Whether you're cornering rival book club captains or unveiling your 12-point plan for global domination, your evil laugh is your punctuation mark. It's the audible equivalent of fireworks.

But you don't become laughter royalty overnight. Crafting a signature cackle takes time, effort, and a throat lozenge or two (but no tears; dictators don't cry). By the end of this chapter, you'll have perfected a laugh so iconic that children, coworkers, and exes will hear it in their nightmares for decades to come.

The Anatomy of an Evil Laugh

Before we jump into how to perfect it, we must dissect it. The evil laugh has three crucial elements, each as vital as your expertly tailored cape. Ignore any of these components, and you risk sounding like a badly maintained car rather than a force of darkness.

- **The Build-Up:** The moment of suspense when your audience isn't sure if you're about to chuckle or full-on lose your mind. The secret here is timing—leave them hanging just long enough for a hint of awkwardness.
- **The Crescendo:** This is where you pour all your malevolent energy into the laugh. Go big, go loud, and make sure it

carries across the room (or at least to the back of the Zoom conference).
- **The Denouement:** The sinister fade-out. Your laugh should never just *stop*. It should trail off like an ominous storm disappearing over the horizon—or like someone remembering they left the stove on.

How-To Guide to Evil Laugh Mastery

Step 1 – Find Your Style

There's no one-size-fits-all evil laugh (though if there were, it would obviously include capes). Your laugh needs to reflect your personality, mission, and daily caffeine intake. Start by picking a category that sets the tone for your villainous persona.

The Classic Villain Laugh ("Muahaha!"):

Timeless and versatile, this laugh is perfect for dictators who live for the drama. It's bold, instantly recognisable, and pairs perfectly with finger-steepling. Example user? Dr. Evil. If it worked for an inter-galactic billionaire with a mini-me sidekick, it'll work for you.

The Mad Scientist Giggle ("Hehehe!"):

A little unhinged, completely theatrical. This one suggests you've crossed the line and *love it*. Think of it as the laugh for those with more chaotic energy than concrete plans. Bonus points if you throw in a snort.

The Sardonic Chuckle ("Hmph-heh!"):

Understated yet devastatingly effective. This is for villains who rule with subtlety and don't have time to yell—because they're too busy sipping espresso in a glass office. Stalin would approve. It hides the madness but leaves just enough mystery.

The Banshee Cackle ("AH-HAHAHA!"):

Crazy, deranged, and straight out of a Tim Burton movie. If your persona involves feeling unhinged for dramatic flair (hello, Gaddafi), this is the laugh for you. Just don't forget to breathe between hysteric shrieks.

Step 2 – Record and Analyse

Now that you have your foundation, it's time to put your laugh to the test. Record yourself attempting various sinister chuckles and perform extensive playback analysis. Focus on the following:

- Is the tone guttural enough to rattle windows?
- Does it feel authentic, like you've been saving it for dramatic monologues?
- Does hearing it make even *you* slightly unsettled?

If the answer isn't a resounding "yes," back to the barbarian drawing board you go.

Step 3 – Dial Up the Theatrics

The key to a viral laugh isn't just the sound but the performance behind it. Think hand gestures, facial expressions, and possibly an intimidating backdrop (a throne room? A dimly lit pantry?). Elevate your laugh from "mildly alarming" to "oh no, they're starting Act II."

- **Eye Movements:** Look up and away as if you're whispering, "Yes, destiny," to the heavens.
- **Hand Movements:** Clasp them dramatically as though holding an invisible goblet of victory. Throwing them wide during the laugh crescendo is optional but highly recommended.
- **Posture:** Straighten your back and lean slightly over your victims—er, friends. Dictators do *not* hunch unless it's for a Bond-villain swivel-chair moment.

Step 4 – Practice with an Audience

Laughter, like fine tailoring, needs test runs. Start small, work your way up. Begin with your most easily intimidated acquaintances (family members, the mailman) and escalate to full rooms of people who can't escape (workplace meetings are ideal). If the reaction includes awe, fear, and awkward silence, you're doing it right.

> Why did the dictator fail at comedy?
> Because no one was allowed to laugh at anyone else's jokes.

Real-Life Inspiration

Dr. Evil – The Quintessential Maniacal Chuckle

Few fictional villains have showcased such consistent laugh mastery as Dr. Evil. His "Muahahaha!" style is a masterclass in theatrical rhythm, with just enough pauses to make minions reconsider their summaries.

Lesson Learned: Pacing is key. Don't spill all the evil drama at once—savour it.

Vincent Price – Horror's Creepy Cool Connoisseur

Price built his entire career atop his haunting laugh, used flawlessly in films, voiceovers, and moments of societal distress. His laugh said, "You'll regret inviting me over," in only the most enticing way.

Lesson Learned: Voice control is everything—add texture to your laugh for depth.

Jafar (Aladdin) – Animated Villainy at Its Peak

Jafar's laugh is all about an operatic build-up that crescendos into full-blown mania. Plus, it pairs well with extravagant staff twirling and condescending monologues (things that, frankly, should be part of *your* routine).

Lesson Learned: Don't just laugh—*immerse* yourself in the experience.

Anthony Hopkins – Hannibal Lecter's Lip-smacking Chef's Kiss

Nobody can ever forget the taunting of poor Clarice Starling from behind the security barrier from film world's greatest cannibal connoisseur and the words "fava beans" and "nice chianti" has never struck more terror since.

Lesson Learned: This laugh is a soft snigger but it is so deep it cuts the jugular without you even realising.

Exercises for Evil Laugh Excellence

1. **Mirror Rehearsals:** Stand before your favourite mirror and experiment with different expressions that maximise horrific charm.
2. **Laugh Ladder:** Start with a chuckle, progressively building into your full evil symphony. Stop just short of scaring the neighbours (unless they deserve it).
3. **Audition Tapes:** Record five variations of your cackle, then play them during awkward public situations like elevator rides or post-meeting lulls. Gauge reactions.

Why did the evil overlord sell cushions?
Because his laughs were "cackle-backed"!

Pro Tips for Laugh Legends

- Mix up styles. Alternate between subtle laughs for minor victories and boisterous laughter for major declaration moments. Variety keeps your audience on edge.

- Always laugh after saying something menacing like, "You'll understand... in time" or "Foolish mortals." These statements demand it.
- Avoid nutty laughter when eating bananas. The optics are subpar.

Final Thought – Your Laugh Is Your Legacy

A perfectly crafted evil laugh isn't just a party trick. It's your audible business card, a sonic boom of authority for every room you wander into. From throwing shade at Swan Lake theatregoers to redefining society's vibe at promotional ribbon-cuttings—it's your ultimate signature.

Now go on, ruler-in-the-making. Practice until every triumphant cackle shakes chandeliers and stuns chronically overconfident people. The universe is waiting to hear you roar—or giggle—your way to supremacy!

Chapter 8: The Cult of Personality – Making Them Worship You

Welcome back, aspiring deity of domination! You've mastered fear, loyalty, propaganda, and perfected an evil laugh that could make mirror manufacturers rich. Now, it's time to ascend to dictatorship's highest form—becoming a deity on Earth. That's right, it's time to make people actually *worship* you (and not just because you created the office-wide three-hour meetings). Welcome to the Cult of Personality, where the people don't just love you—they can't imagine life without you.

Crafting a larger-than-life persona isn't for the faint of heart—or the faint of wardrobe (see Chapter 6 for your fabulous fashion guide). This stage requires a cocktail of charisma, manipulation, and shameless self-promotion. You aren't just building a profile; you're designing an icon so blindingly radiant, your narcissism feels like a public service.

When done correctly, you'll have followers declaring eternal devotion over microwaveable pizza, erecting monuments where your ego towers over the skyline, and rewriting history books to explain how you once wrestled hurricanes into submission.

Understanding the Cult of Personality

A "cult of personality" isn't about actual substance—it's about perception. You don't need to be great; you just need people to *think* you are. (Kim Jong-un reportedly "learned to drive" at age three and scaled North Korea's highest peak in designer loafers, so the bar's truly as flexible as your imagination allows.)

The "cult" part means people will view you as some ethereal mix of saviour, superhero, and cosmic chef who blesses the masses with perfectly cooked metaphors. It's your golden moment to shine brighter than the collective rationality of society allows.

How to Build Your Cult of Personality

Step 1 – Give Yourself an Over-the-Top Origin Story

You can't build a godlike persona on top of an ordinary backstory like, "Oh, I have a degree in economics, and my hobbies include gardening." Nope. Your origin story needs mystique, grandeur, and at least three unverifiable yet awe-inspiring events.

Consider these options:

- **Mythical Birth:** Sure, everyone knows you were born in a hospital, but why settle for boring truth when the masses are crying out for legend? Claim your birth was foretold by a solar eclipse or accompanied by a rare alignment of Jupiter's moons. Bonus points if animals "rejoiced" at your arrival.
- **Prodigious Childhood:** You weren't just good at school. You were solving advanced physics equations before breakfast and personally ending neighbourhood squabbles with wisdom beyond your years. "At age four, I ended a sandbox civil war. Coincidence? Hardly."
- **Overcoming Impossible Odds:** Did you emerge triumphant from an utterly fabricated struggle? Craft a tale of rising from misfortune to become the nation's beacon of hope. Poverty, illness, earthquakes—it doesn't matter if the struggles were entirely local weather updates; make yourself the hero.

Pro Tip: Add just enough detail to make it sound plausible to casual listeners but vague enough that no one can actually verify it.

Step 2 – Master the Art of Relatable Superiority

The key to being worshipped is to balance humility with otherworldly confidence. You want people to think, "Wow, they're just like me... but better, obviously." You need to become that untouchable hybrid of

Oprah, Chairman Mao, and Zeus, radiating brilliance while showing *just enough* humanity to be loveable.

- **Staged "Everyman" Moments:** Be seen doing things "normal" people do, like eating ice cream cones or playing with a puppy. (Note: The puppy should be perfect. Choose a golden retriever and definitely avoid chihuahuas; their chaos undermines your serenity.)
- **Humble Bragging:** Casually mention achievements like, "Oh, I had no idea this speech would inspire world peace—it was just a doodle I jotted between solving global energy crises." Be humble, but not really.
- **Show 'Imperfections' Strategically:** Admire how history books claim Napoleon was short (he wasn't particularly.) Find or invent a flaw for yourself—it makes people think you're relatable, even if that flaw is something ridiculous like "I eat *too many* health foods."

Step 3 – Commission Awe-Inducing Imagery

Holy artwork, Batman—you need visuals! You're not a deity until your face is plastered on posters, murals, and potentially snack packaging. Every city should have your 12-foot likeness glowering confidently toward the horizon.

- **Posters for the Public:** Invest in full-colour posters of yourself doing heroic things like rescuing cats from trees, solving household plumbing issues, or gesturing dramatically at distant landscapes.
- **Statues:** Start small—maybe a tasteful bust in a library. Work your way up to a monument where pigeons will one day perch on your iconic nose. If you're daring, opt for something interactive, like Stalin's rotating globe or Kim Il-Sung's

technicolour flower-filled towers.
- **Iconography:** Transform your likeness into a logo. Perhaps your profile in dramatic shadow or an outstretched hand that symbolises generosity (and dominion). Don't overthink it—Apple did the same with fruit and look how that turned out.

Step 4 – Deliver Statements Bathed in Gravitas

Every word out of your mouth needs the weight of prophecy. People shouldn't merely hear you speak; they should *witness* it like it's the Second Coming of Shakespeare meets Beyoncé's halftime show.

- Replace common phrases with florid pseudo-poetry, e.g., "It will rain tomorrow" becomes "The heavens have consulted, and their tears will quench the Earth's thirst at dawn."
- Speak slowly, as if your words were firsthand carved into stone tablets by angels. Long pauses are your best friend; they add drama to even the most mundane observations.
- Never answer direct questions. Redirect with statements like, "I think what we *really* need to ask is how I continue to inspire everyone every day."

Bonus tip? Cultivate a catchphrase. Something simple yet profound that works in every scenario, like, "Everything begins with me." Because, obviously, it does.

Step 5 – Rewrite Reality

True figureheads of worship don't merely exist in the present—they redefine the past and future. Your legacy isn't just what you *do*—it's what you convince people you've already done.

- Commission elaborate stories of your benevolence solving

natural disasters. "Remember that volcano that didn't erupt? You're welcome."
- Modify historical events. Did you invent the internet? According to your reprinted biographies, yes. Did photos exist of someone else? Photoshop (or just wipe them altogether).
- Rename things! Cities, highways, lunar craters—it's all fair game. Very soon, no major landmark should lack your personal stamp.

Why don't dictators ever get lost?

Because they always take the *right* turn. (And all the other turns are banned.)

Real-Life Inspiration – Idolized Individuals

Kim Jong-un – The Man, The Myth, The Legend

Kim's larger-than-life persona isn't an accident. His propaganda machine pumps out stories of jaw-dropping accomplishments (the aforementioned childhood driving feat, anyone?) and claims so extraordinary, they'd make Aesop blush.

Lesson Learned: People can only question your claims so much before they just shrug and throw flowers at your feet.

Muammar Gaddafi – The Self-Proclaimed "Guide of the Revolution"

Gaddafi rebranded himself as the *saviour* of Libya, sprinkling revolution speeches with theatrics and always finding the camera's best angle. Statue? Check. Entire "Green Book" policies? Double-check.

Lesson Learned: If people don't remember the policies, at least make sure they remember the outfits.

Chairman Mao – Literally Everywhere

Mao Zedong's face was as unavoidable as oxygen during his reign. From propaganda posters to literature, those eyes were watching *everything*.
Lesson Learned: Visibility equals immortality.

And many more!

Check out the Compendium of Dictators at the end of this book!

Exercises for Building Worshipful Obsession

1. **Write Your Origin Film Script:** Draft the movie version of your life that leaves out reality's dull bits. Hire imaginary A-list actors to play you. Viola Davis is a solid choice.
2. **Create Your Signature Pose:** Find a stance that oozes confidence and make it your official imagery—arm raised; chin slightly tilted. Practicing before a wind machine is non-negotiable.
3. **Launch Your Own Hashtag:** Something along the lines of #HailTheBoss. Start small. Before you know it, school kids will graffiti it across bus stops.

Pro Tips

- **Smile**. Not often—just enough that when you *do*, it feels like a solar eclipse broke just for you.
- **Always reference yourself in the third person** during speeches. Exhaust them psychologically until they say it for you.
- **Build an anthem**. Dictators with jingles last longer; it's science.

Final Thought

Building a cult of personality takes shamelessness, imagination, and the complete abandonment of humility—the holy trifecta of effective dictatorial leadership. But your reward is eternal adoration (or, at the very least, eternal toleration).

Now think big. Brighter. Bigger.

Go forth and make monuments rise, hashtags trend, and nations tremble when they pronounce your name. Because after all, what's a dynasty without a deity?

Chapter 9: Handling Rebellion – Crushing Dissent with Style

Welcome back, powerhouse of oppression and glory! Thus far, you've conquered hearts, minds, and wardrobes. But what about those pesky rebels who dare to speak up, question your brilliance, or—*gasp*—suggest improvements to your policies? Rebels are the pricks in the perfectly inflated ego of dictatorship, and unfortunately, they tend to multiply faster than your propaganda team can churn out flattering photo opps.

Fear not, for rebellion is as much a ruler's rite of passage as constructing a giant, unnecessary statue of yourself. Think of it as the universe's way of checking if you're still worthy of the iron-fist crown. And *of course* you are. All you need is a strategy that balances absurd ruthlessness with enough pizzazz to keep the masses entertained—or at least distracted.

By the end of this chapter, you'll have mastered the art of stomping out dissent while looking so effortlessly fabulous, it'll be hard for anyone to decide whether they're terrified or in awe.

Understanding Rebellion – What's Their Deal?

Before you squish your opposition like a bug under your luxurious Christian Louboutin boots, it's worth knowing why rebellions exist. Not because you care (obviously not), but because knowledge is power—and power is your currency.

Why Do People Rebel?

1. **Inequality** – Peasants love complaining when they don't have as much gold-plated cutlery as you. Ungrateful.
2. **Oppression** – Apparently, some people value their "freedom"

over your perfectly curated laws. Disrespectful.
3. **Personal Grudges** – That one time you stole someone's parking spot or declared their village a "non-essential" zone. Petty.
4. **General Chaos Enthusiasts** – There are always a few who just enjoy the drama of dissent, like over-caffeinated bloggers hunting for retweets.

Your goal isn't to argue or reason with these folks. You're a dictator, not their therapist. Your job is to recognise rebellion as the amateur hour that it is and crush it with the gravitas of a seasoned overlord.

The Stylish Art of Squashing Rebellion

Step 1 – Spin the Narrative

First things first, *nobody must know you're rattled*. Rebellion? What rebellion? You're not fighting dissenters; you're dealing with ungrateful citizens who "simply don't understand your vision."

- **Cast Yourself as the Victim:** Use every microphone in sight to declare, "Look at the burdens I bear for you! And this is how you repay me?" Throw in some tears for bonus effect—make sure they glisten like diamonds under stage lighting.
- **Create a Scapegoat:** Blame the unrest on something convenient—foreign powers, natural disasters, or TikTok trends. Nobody should believe for a second that it's *your* fault.
- **Flip the Script:** Describe rebels as *anti-you*—not visionary saviours of the people, but irritants trying to dismantle your legacy. Use terms like "traitors," "saboteurs," or if you're feeling modern, "fake news generators."

Pro Tip: Shift the blame to a previously unknown subgroup. "The Alliance of Shirtless Canaries" has a nice ominous ring to it and nobody can prove they *don't* exist.

Step 2 – Distract, Dazzle, and Divide

Once you've denied the rebellion's validity, it's time to redirect everyone's attention to something shinier and less treacherous.

- **Throw a Parade:** Nothing diffuses tension like free hot dogs and a stage covered in glitter cannons. Declare the rebellion irrelevant by hosting the nation's largest party. Bonus points if there's a live band composed of *mandatory volunteers*.
- **Announce a New "People-centred" Initiative:** Introduce policies like "National Pancake Day" or a ban on Mondays. The goal is to make citizens too giddy or bamboozled to keep chanting slogans.
- **Divide and Conquer:** Identify factions within the rebellion and turn them against each other. A whispered rumour here, a bribe there, and suddenly their movement implodes like a soufflé during an earthquake. Nobody can rebel when they're too busy fighting among themselves.

Step 3 – Discredit the Rebels

Rebels rely on credibility, so your job is to turn their public image into literal rubble. It's not defamation—it's practical leadership!

- **Label Them with Unflattering Titles:** Words like "terrorist," "villain," or "hooligans" pack a punch. For lesser offenders, consider "losers" or "uninspired tweeters."
- **Highlight Their Weaknesses:** "Oh, you don't trust me, the glorious protector of snacks? Well, Bob over there failed algebra twice and occasionally eats soup directly from the

can. Whose judgment will you trust?"
- **Invent Scandals:** Nobody follows a rebel leader accused of stealing library books or wearing socks with sandals. Fabricate their downfall with flair!

<u>Pro Tip:</u> Mock them openly. "I would take this rebellion seriously if their banner didn't look like it was drawn by angry toddlers."

Step 4 – Deploy Style-Savvy Suppression

Things escalating? No problem! You'll need to flex your muscle, but don't forget to accessorise your iron fist. If you're going to crush dissent, do it with style.

- **Send a Message:** Symbolic gestures are key. A dictator-approved "message" can include revoking privileges (like Wi-Fi access) or renaming rebel landmarks after yourself. How does "Supreme Leader Boulevard and Gift Shop" sound?
- **Invent Playful Victories:** Did someone knock over a light post in a rebellion stronghold? Declare it a win. Caption your social media posts with "Rebels brought down like this lamp."
- **Public Displays of Authority:** Coordinate your army's march not just with precision, but with *choreography*. Throw in a custom soundtrack. Everyone loves a properly timed drumbeat.

Never forget, the act of suppression must look so fabulous that people hesitate to rebel next time solely to avoid competing with your theatrical dominance.

Step 5 – Re-educate with Pizazz

Crushing rebellion isn't just about stopping dissent—it's about ensuring it doesn't pop back like an uncooperative zit. That means reconditioning the masses to believe resisting you is somewhere between futile and mildly uncool.

- **Offer "Rehabilitation Clinics":** Convert dissenters into loyalists by introducing re-education programs disguised as wellness retreats. Bonus points for providing comfy robes and fresh-pressed propaganda materials in the welcome kit.
- **Use Groupthink:** Encourage mass displays of allegiance. Gather citizens to paint a mural of your face, or stage synchronized "random" chants of your excellence. Peer pressure works wonders!
- **Reward Compliance, lavishly:** Ensure loyalty feels more enticing than rebellion. Hand out medals (stamped with your face, obviously) to anyone whose support is particularly theatrical.

Real-Life Inspiration

Idi Amin – The Charm and Chaos Balance

Idi Amin crushed opposition like a man reinventing whack-a-mole, but with occasional PR pivots that involved gifts to foreign leaders and endless self-promotion. His ability to appear both lovable and terrifying remains a dictator's case study.

Lesson Learned: Always smile for the camera—even if your opponent is tied up behind it.

Saddam Hussein – The World's Most Micromanaged Suppression

Saddam's secret police were notoriously effective, but it was his flair for publicized strength (and endless portraits of himself) that ensured rebellion remained... inconvenient at best.

Lesson Learned: Micromanaging isn't just for bad bosses—it's for bad sovereigns too.

And many more!

Check out the Compendium of Dictators at the end of this book!

Exercises for Aspiring Suppressors

1. **Write a Rebel's Tell-All:** Draft a fake memoir in which rebel leaders secretly admire you. Make it absurdly dramatic and read excerpts at public events.
2. **Stage a Suppression Fashion Show:** Host an event where your security forces showcase their tailored uniforms. Add a category for "Best Intimidating Pose."
3. **Invent a Symbol of Your Victory:** Declare the pineapple (or some equally random object) your symbol of strength. Rebellions can't possibly beat the fruit king/queen.

Pro Tips

- Always suppress rebellions during prime time. Late-night crushing is so passé.
- Never underestimate the power of humour—mock rebels with exaggerated skits.
- Keep a "rebel snack budget" to bribe outliers with artisanal cheeses.

Why did the autocrat hate gardening?
Because he couldn't stand the idea of *power* going to the *roots*.

Final Thought

Rebellions happen to the best of us. What separates amateurs from professionals is how you suppress them—with grace, flair, and an unrelenting amount of ego. Remember, you're not just shutting down dissent; you're reminding the world why you rule better than a thousand rebels combined.

Go forth, glorious suppressor, and stomp rebellion with style—and, if possible, a top hat. Because rebellion may be eternal, but so is your fabulous reign.

Chapter 10: Propaganda and Image Control

Congratulations, aspiring Supreme Leader! If you've made it this far, you're undoubtedly on your way to becoming a well-dressed, fear-inducing icon with an evil laugh so perfectly executed, it could terrify garden gnomes. But there's one crucial element left in your dictatorial toolkit—crafting a public image so immaculate, so carefully filtered, that not even Nostradamus himself could predict a flaw. That's where propaganda and image control come in.

Yes, in this shiny dystopia of your making, the truth is whatever *you* want it to be. Facts? Optional. Reality? Adaptable. Your job is to flood every corner of society with the narrative of **you**. You're not just a person—you're the sun, the stars, and whatever Instagram filter makes life look ten times better than it really is. And the best part? No one must suspect otherwise.

By the end of this chapter, you'll be bending media to your will, rewriting history like an overzealous Wikipedia editor, and curating a personal brand so polished that Beyoncé would take notes.

The Golden Rule of Propaganda

Repeat after me, darling despot-in-training: **Control the message; control the masses.**

Propaganda is the velvet glove on your iron fist. It's how you sell ideas, suppress dissent, and convince millions that you *did* in fact personally raise the GDP by 300% simply by gracing an agricultural field with your dazzling presence. Whether it's through posters, speeches, or TikTok (yes, even tyrants must evolve), you must drip-feed the people a constant diet of curated narratives.

And remember, subtlety is overrated. If anyone accuses you of being over the top, smile and say, "I can't hear you over the sound of my exceptional legacy."

The Mechanics of Perfect Propaganda

Step 1 – Craft the Narrative

Building a rock-solid propaganda foundation starts with asking one simple question: **What version of reality do you want people to believe?**

Do you want to be seen as a benevolent visionary? A fearless warrior? The *only* human who understands economics, rocket science, and how to perfectly cook risotto? Pick your theme and stick to it harder than cling wrap on Tupperware.

- **The Savior:** You are the one who personally saved the nation from poverty, invaders, and expired yogurt. Without you, chaos would reign.
- **The Genius:** Did you invent electricity? No? Who cares! Rewrite history so you did and throw in some made-up patents while you're at it.
- **The Protector:** Oh, the world out there is so scary, but lucky for everyone, they have *you* to defend them from vague existential threats.

Whatever story you choose, make sure it's big, bold, and absolutely unprovable. If people can't question it, they can't defeat it.

Step 2 – Control the Media

The media is your greatest ally—or your worst nightmare if you don't get a chokehold on it early. Unsure how to do this? Don't worry, my little Machiavellian butterfly, I've got you covered.

1. **Own It:** Start by nationalizing all news outlets. Why bother convincing journalists when you can simply *be* their boss? Suddenly, every puff piece and breaking bulletin is dripping with your name.
2. **Flood the Market:** Saturate all channels with your narrative. Billboards, radio jingles, 24/7 news coverage…and for a modern twist, an influencer campaign wouldn't hurt either. Imagine TikTok dances in your honour (hashtag "#DictatorGoals").
3. **Silencing the Spoilsports:** For those pesky independent voices who refuse to cooperate, kindly show them the door—or, better yet, show them the dungeon. (For legal and PR purposes, call it a "media rehabilitation space.")

<u>Pro Tip:</u> Commission your own film studio. Who needs Hollywood when you can produce multi-million-dollar blockbusters about your *fictional* accomplishments, complete with CGI explosions and orchestral scores?

Step 3 – Redesign Reality

Here's the trick about controlling your image—you don't have to align with actual events. Facts are like raw dough; they're meant to be shaped.

- **Edit Your History:** Every biography about you should read like a Marvel origin story. Edit out the unflattering parts (like that awkward karaoke night from college) and add in a few "miraculous" incidents.
- **Delete the Unhelpful:** Obsolete monuments? Gone. Historical photos that contradict your narrative? Photoshop them, burn them, and then Photoshop the ashes.
- **Rename Everything:** Nothing says "I own this place" like

renaming streets, schools, and even animals after yourself. Imagine the majesty of Supreme Leader Salmon or Victory Avenue (Now With 500% More Dictator).

Pro Tip: Install propaganda statues where pigeons *can't* poop on them. The optics are critical.

Step 4 – Appeal to Emotion

Propaganda doesn't work because it's rational—it works because it's emotional. Your job is to make people feel something, even if that something is 99% manufactured nonsense.

1. **Fear:** Create enemies where none exist. "The war on poorly cooked noodles is real, and only I can save you!"
2. **Hope:** Promise the moon, the stars, and maybe a golden retriever puppy for every household. It doesn't matter if it's feasible; the vision is enough.
3. **Pride:** Convince them that supporting you makes them part of something greater than themselves. People will tolerate a lot when they think they're in the "in" crowd.

Pro Tip: Throw in a heartwarming story about how you personally helped a villager with their harvest. Did it happen? Who cares—it'll bring tears to their eyes.

Step 5 – Stay Omni-Present

The ultimate goal is that people can't wake up, take a breath, or eat a sad office lunch without being reminded of your greatness. Here are some foolproof techniques:

- **Portrait Placement:** Your face goes *everywhere*, from banknotes to coffee cups to reusable grocery totes.

(Environmentally responsible dictatorship is *in*.)
- **Nationalized Slogans:** Replace generic sayings with tailored propaganda gems like, "Teamwork is great, but obedience is better!"
- **Themed Days in Your Honor:** Birthdays, anniversaries, "casual Thursdays"... Any excuse to remind people that oxygen itself is possible only because of you.

Greatest Hits of Global Propagandists

Joseph Goebbels – The PhD of Propaganda

Goebbels turned Nazi propaganda into an art form (albeit horrifyingly evil art). His techniques of saturating every medium with mind-numbing repetition proved that a big enough lie, repeated often, could become fact.

Lesson Learned: Hammer. It. Home. If anyone forgets your message, even for a second, you're slacking.

North Korea – Rewriting Geography

The North Korean propaganda machine spares no effort in presenting Kim Jong-un as a near-divine figure who can fly, moonwalk, and possibly defeat the Avengers solo.

Lesson Learned: The more absurd the claim, the harder it is to argue.

Napoleon – It's All About the Symbols

Napoleon mastered imagery, plastering his name, face, and initials across emblems, shields, and probably the occasional camembert wheel. He made himself unavoidable, even post-downfall.

Lesson Learned: People should see you everywhere—whether they like it or not.

And many more!

Check out the Compendium of Dictators at the end of this book!

Exercises for the Aspiring Propaganda Guru

1. **Write Your Own Wikipedia Page:** Include wildly exaggerated claims, like winning high school "Most Likely to Save Civilisation" or founding the concept of brunch.
2. **Design a Personal Logo:** Think symbols of grandeur—an eagle riding a lion, a flaming crown, or a single teardrop symbolizing how beautiful you are under pressure.
3. **Invent Inspiring Hashtags:** Nothing says "modern despot" like #BossDictator or #ObeyAndSlay trending worldwide.

Pro Tips for Dictatorial Branding

- Never apologise. A true ruler makes no mistakes, only "unexpected creative pivots."
- Always have a motto. Something like, *"Because I said so"* or *"Unity through me.*"* (Subtle, yet effective.)
- Memorise this phrase for interviews: "This isn't propaganda; it's the truth, amplified."

What's a dictator's favourite game?
Follow the Leader—because everyone has to play by his rules.

Final Thought – You Are the Brand

Nobody said dictatorship would be humble, and with propaganda on your side, it doesn't have to be. Flood the media with your face, your voice, and your greatness until nobody can imagine a world without you running the show—or at least narrating it. Strap in, Supreme Leader, and start spinning reality into your biggest achievement yet.

Because remember, if the truth doesn't flatter you... well, who needs it?

Chapter 11: Eliminating the Opposition – Clearing the Path to Absolute Power

Congratulations, ambitious autocrat! You made it to the part of your dictatorial adventure where the gloves come off—metaphorically, of course. You wouldn't want to ruin those impeccable designer pairs you picked up after implementing your suggested retail therapy in Chapter 6. Now, it's time to clean house. By house, we mean your entire government, workplace, and possibly that one neighbourhood HOA board that still doesn't think the statue of you fits their landscaping aesthetics.

The opposition—a.k.a. those irritating fellow humans who refuse to bask in your godlike radiance without muttering snide remarks under their breath—doesn't eliminate itself. This step requires strategy, flair, and maybe a faint whiff of popcorn-worthy drama. After all, if you're going to crush your rivals, you might as well make it a spectacle. Because nothing says power like disposing of your enemies while the masses cheer, "Best. Show. *Ever.*"

By the end of this chapter, you'll learn how to identify threats, neutralise them with ease (and maybe a flash of style), and turn eliminating opposition into an art form worthy of its own TED Talk. If Stalin could rewrite friendship as a career-ending mistake, so can you.

Why Eliminate the Opposition?

Because they exist, obviously. But if we need to get philosophical, here's why dealing with dissenters is critical to your reign of unparalleled glory.

1. **They Threaten Your Narrative.** Nobody invited their conflicting ideologies to the party. If their ideas don't align with yours, they might as well not exist—and soon, they

won't.
2. **They Sap Your Aura.** How can you focus on ruling with glittering magnificence if someone keeps disagreeing with every decree? They're ruining the vibe, and that's unforgivable.
3. **It's a Rite of Passage.** No dictator worth their gold-leaf palace goes through their entire tenure without knocking a few opposing players off the chessboard. This is *the* milestone that separates amateurs from legends.

The Art of Opposition Eradication

Step 1 – Identify Your Threats

You can't squash your enemies if you don't know who they are. Of course, in this paranoid-style environment you've likely fostered, *everyone* is a potential threat. How's that for efficiency? But to truly weed out opposition, start by categorising your enemies.

- **The Ambitious Rival:** They're sharp-dressed, sharp-tongued, and always a little too comfortable occupying the seat next to you at meetings.
- **The Subversive Whiner:** This delightful specimen questions your every move. They have "know-it-all at Thanksgiving" energy and must be silenced.
- **The Popular Rebel:** Charisma magnet, saviour complex—you know exactly who to hate, and so does everyone else. Spoiler alert: Being more likeable than you is punishable by... well, you'll see.

<u>Pro Tip:</u> Keep things interesting by inventing non-existent foes. Blame blunders, missing office supplies, or drops in national fish supply on fabricated enemies. It's not paranoia if it works.

Step 2 – Employ Divide and Conquer

Why eliminate a united opposition when you can ensure they destroy themselves like bickering reality TV contestants? The key is sowing mistrust and infighting among your rivals.

- **Start Rumours:** Did The Ambitious Rival just admit to never washing their coffee mug? Spread that delicious titbit around the office—or, you know, the national media.
- **Grant and Revoke Favors at Random:** Elevate one opponent and then smack them back to obscurity while elevating their colleague. They'll be too focused on playing musical chairs to bother you.
- **Secret Alliances:** Befriend one enemy to take down another. Of course, you will eventually eliminate the first enemy too (bonus points for intrigue).

<u>Pro Tip:</u> Never trust anyone who says, "It's just business." That person is plotting your downfall while filming TikToks about your unfortunate haircut last week.

Step 3 – Opt for Theatrical Eliminations

Sometimes subtlety is overrated. You're not just removing threats; you're crafting *moments*. History remembers bold strokes, not quiet boardroom firings.

- **Show Trials:** What better way to demonstrate your power than by scripting a courtroom drama where the antagonist is always guilty? Bonus points for crocodile tears and melodramatic gasps from the gallery.
- **Public Humiliations:** Did someone dare send a strongly worded memo against you? Well, it just so happens you booked a stadium to host their impromptu apology.

- **Unsolvable Exiles:** Send opposers somewhere suitably poetic—like a faraway island or a never-ending escape room. DIY creativity is half the fun! Imagine banishing someone to "unmoderated online forums."

Pro Tip: When staging their "downfall," don't forget your camera crew. If you're going viral, make it fabulous.

Step 4 – Silence the Rumblings

Once you've cleaned house, make sure no one dares to whisper opposition again. Here's how to ensure aftermath control is sleek and secure.

- **Rewrite the Narrative:** That popular rival who mysteriously disappeared? Declare they were never important anyway, citing obscure historical revisions only *you* have access to.
- **Invent New Enemies:** If people don't have an opposing figure to hate, they might notice how many disappearances you've had. Redirect their fury toward imaginary traitors.
- **Document Your Mercy:** Announce that contrary to *fake news*, you gave The Subversive Whiner a cushy "retirement." Never mind what retirement means in this case.

Pro Tip: Consider hiring a team of "actors" to explain to the public how they feel TOTALLY fine now working in your...uh...redevelopment centres.

Real-Life Lessons in Power Clearing

Josef Stalin – The Purge Prodigy

Stalin took enemy elimination to Olympic levels. With ruthless efficiency and impressive theatrics, he made dissent a thing of the past (sometimes literally overnight). Friends weren't safe, comrades were disposable, and nobody dared play Monopoly with him for fear of "suspicious strategies."

Lesson Learned: Paranoia is free. Use it liberally. And always pack extra gulags for emergencies.

Kim Jong-un – Family's Fair Game

Kim Jong-un showed us that *even family's* not off-limits if you have a regime. One mysterious disappearance after another (allegedly!) proved that power knows no blood ties—well, no permanent ones, anyway.

Lesson Learned: Keep your Christmas guest list short and always have an exit strategy (for others).

Margaret Thatcher – All the Sass, No Assassinations

The Iron Lady didn't physically eliminate her opposition, but she outmanoeuvred critics with biting one-liners and unwavering dominance. Proof that sometimes, you can squash dissent with words sharper than any sword.

Lesson Learned: If wit doesn't work, revert to exile and fireworks.

And many more!

Check out the Compendium of Dictators at the end of this book!

Exercises for Aspiring Rival Removers

1. **The "Name List" Exercise:** Write down 10 names of possible rivals tonight. Tomorrow, write another list since paranoia breeds creativity.
2. **Opposition Bingo:** Design a card where each square represents a fantastical fate for enemies ("sent to study

penguins in Antarctica" or "hired as my new footstool").
3. **Practice Speechifying:** Stand in front of a mirror and rehearse, "I had to make the hard choice... for YOU!" Make it Oscar-worthy.

Pro Tips for Efficient Elimination

- Never act predictably. Rivals relax when you're predictable, so become the human embodiment of jazz improvisation (chaos is your forté).
- Always keep spare alibis in case things get "messy."
- Celebrate your victories. Host a "National Day of Fewer Losers" once in a while—it's cathartic and fantastic branding.

Why did the autocrat start a bakery?
He wanted to control the dough.

Final Thought – Stay Unmatched

No one said eliminating opposition would be easy—or bloodless. But remember, it's not just about clearing obstacles. It's about cementing your legend with mind-blowing efficacy and dramatic flair. Go forth, oh Sovereign of Strategised Sabotage, and turn your rivals into distant footnotes—preferably in books about your overarching magnificence. The throne is always comfier without extra opinions rattling around.

Chapter 12: The Dictator's Retirement Plan – Bowing Out with Panache

Congratulations, illustrious overlord! You've built a regime that would make Machiavelli dab with pride, crushed rebellions with style, perfected propaganda to Kardashian levels, and eliminated rivals so thoroughly they might as well have been wiped from the fabric of space-time. But now it's time for the question no dictator likes to think about: **What next?**

No one lives forever (not even you, Supreme Exemplar of Perfection). At some point, even the most iron-fisted leader must hang up their epaulets and decide whether to retire to a villa in the Mediterranean or vanish in dramatic fashion, leaving conspiracy theories in your wake. Retirement, believe it or not, isn't just for overworked office drones—it's also for you, almighty tyrant. The key is to retire on your own terms, with as much grace, flair, and self-serving legacy-building as possible.

By the end of this chapter, you'll not only have a foolproof retirement strategy (because who's going to say otherwise?) but also the ultimate exit that guarantees you're remembered fondly—or at least fearfully.

Step 1 – Decide Your Exit Strategy

Retirement for dictators isn't quite as simple as clearing out your desk and joining a shuffleboard league. You've got to think bigger. Here are some classic options for your transition, each with its own touch of pizzazz.

The Grand Disappearing Act

There's something undeniably sexy about vanishing from the public eye with no explanation. One day you're ruling with an iron fist; the next, you're gone. Did you flee to a secret island? Fake your death? Ascend to heaven on a golden chariot? The beauty of this approach is the speculation—it keeps your name (and memes about you) alive for eternity.

- **How to Pull It Off:** Stage an elaborate helicopter getaway during a "routine inspection" of your holdings. Leave an ominous note behind, like "The truth lies beneath the pyramid of power."
- **Historical Highlight:** Kim Jong-Il orchestrated propaganda about his death so overwhelmingly absurd (rainbows, birds singing his praises) that one might think he became a deity in the afterlife.

The "Senior Statesman" Pivot

If you're feeling less theatrical, you could pivot to a quieter life as an "elder statesman," offering unsolicited advice to political up-and-comers or hosting lavish conferences where you regale attendees with tales of your glorious reign.

- **How to Pull It Off:** Build a think tank, preferably named after yourself (*The Supreme Harmony Institute sounds nice*). Publish a memoir so nauseatingly self-congratulatory it doubles as a drinking game for historians.
- **Historical Highlight:** Augusto Pinochet transitioned from dictator to... slightly less hands-on dictator in semi-retirement. Sure, the man wasn't winning International

Grandpa of the Year awards, but hey, he remained *relevant*!

The Democratic "Rebranding"

For those dictators who crave applause for their magnanimity, there's always the option of staging an ostentatious handover of power to a "democratic" successor (read: your successor, puppet, sibling, or clone). This allows you to retire as a hero while continuing to hold the real power behind the scenes like a shadowy puppeteer with God complex tendencies.

- **How to Pull It Off:** Announce free elections that are handily won by your designated stooge. Bonus points for writing glowing analysis pieces about "your nation's democratic transformation" under a pseudonym.
- **Historical Highlight:** Vladimir Putin and Dmitry Medvedev's dramatic game of presidential musical chairs fooled no one and continues to deliver wild season finales.

The Lavish Exile

If the heat gets too intense and your charm's lost on the citizens, exile can actually be a rather comfortable retirement option. Sure, you're technically banished, but with enough embezzled funds, you can afford a mansion where even your enemies would RSVP immediately to your housewarming party.

- **How to Pull It Off:** Choose a tax-haven nation, preferably one with lax extradition laws. Announce you're retiring for "health reasons," conveniently forgetting to mention that the public would gleefully chase you with pitchforks if you stayed.

- **Historical Highlight:** Baby Doc Duvalier famously took his stolen millions to Europe, enjoying luxury while the peasants back home scratched their heads and muttered, "Wait, did we... win?"

Step 2 – Lay the Groundwork

No good exit plan happens overnight. Whether you're vanishing like Houdini or orchestrating a handpicked handover, the key is preparation, darling.

1. Cultivate Your Legacy

Start working on your greatest role yet—benevolent hero of history. Commission statues, write "official" biographies, and, if possible, rename a small constellation after yourself.

Pro Tip: If sculptors keep capturing your bad side, hire a photoshop-savvy millennial to "correct" history.

2. Hoard Resources

Remain fabulous in exile by making sure a few billion dollars conveniently vanish into Swiss bank accounts or cryptocurrency wallets before your "retirement." Don't get too greedy, though—leave something behind so future leaders have a country *to* lead.

Pro Tip: Diversify! Cash is great, but yachts, vineyards, and rare Pokémon cards hold value too.

3. Create a Scapegoat

Before you leave, pin the nation's problems on someone else. That way, if things go south, the masses don't come chasing after you with flaming torches. Choose carefully disposable allies, rival nations, or even the concept of gravity work wonders.

Step 3 – Plan a "Post-Retirement" Hustle

Just because you're stepping down doesn't mean your influence ends. Here are some hobbies to keep you busy.

- **Orchestrate Puppetry:** From behind the scenes, ensure your policies remain law—no matter who's officially in charge.
- **Join the Speaking Circuit:** Nothing says "retired dictator" like charging $200,000 per keynote to explain how *you alone* solved world hunger.
- **Launch a Lifestyle Brand:** Sure, you ruled a nation, but why not rule the fitness or skincare industry next? Kim Jong-un walking this path with K-pop-esque hair tutorials would break the internet.

Exercises for Your Retirement Plan

1. **Draft Your Farewell Speech:** Make it dripping with fake humility and vague promises, like "I have chosen to pass the torch—not because it's heavy, but because my greatness is too blinding."
2. **Design Your Beach Villa:** Sketch out where the gold-plated infinity pool will go. Doesn't your jacuzzi deserve to overlook *two* oceans?
3. **Practice Signatures:** Refine your autograph for signing checks, memoirs, and the rare fan letter.

Notable Retirees to Pin on Your Vision Board

- **Fidel Castro:** Retired but kept showing up occasionally, like a political groundhog—long enough to remind everyone he

was still in charge.
- **Cincinnatus:** The dictator nobody really remembers because he gave up power VOLUNTARILY. What are you doing in this list, Cincy? Move it along.
- **Napoleon:** Retired (well, exiled) not once but *twice*. Proof that even in retirement, you can still leave room for an epic comeback tour.

What's a dictator's favourite social media platform?
MySpace—because it's all about him.

Final Thought – Leave Them Wanting More

Retirement as a dictator isn't about fading into obscurity—it's about staging your exit so brilliantly that people can't stop talking about it for centuries. Whether it's vanishing amid conspiracies, mentoring from the shadows, or sipping Mai Tais while the world debates your legacy, your endgame deserves all the drama and flair your rule embodied.

Remember, the only thing more powerful than being in control... is being unforgettable. Cheers to retirement! Bring sunscreen—you've earned it.

Chapter 13: A Short Compendium of the Very Worst

Here's a list of 20 individuals widely regarded as notorious dictators, spanning historical and contemporary periods. The useful steps in this book have been inspired by their stories, their infamy and headcount. The epitome of "masculine energy" that the Zuckerbergs, Bezoses and Musks and other garden variety of broligarchs rave about. Here they are again in the glorious and goriest of detail:

1. **Adolf Hitler (Germany):** Leader of Nazi Germany, responsible for the Holocaust and World War II.
2. **Joseph Stalin (Soviet Union):** Dictator of the Soviet Union, responsible for mass purges, forced famines, and the Gulag system.
3. **Mao Zedong (China):** Chairman of the Chinese Communist Party, whose policies led to widespread famine and political persecution.
4. **Pol Pot (Cambodia):** Leader of the Khmer Rouge, responsible for the Cambodian genocide.
5. **Kim Il-sung (North Korea):** Founder of North Korea, establishing a totalitarian regime.
6. **Benito Mussolini (Italy):** Leader of fascist Italy.
7. **Idi Amin (Uganda):** Dictator of Uganda, known for his brutal regime and human rights abuses.
8. **Augusto Pinochet (Chile):** Dictator of Chile, responsible for widespread human rights violations.
9. **Saddam Hussein (Iraq):** Dictator of Iraq, known for his brutal rule and use of chemical weapons.
10. **Francisco Franco (Spain):** Dictator of Spain, who came to power after the Spanish Civil War.
11. **Vladimir Lenin (Russia):** Leader of the Bolshevik

revolution, and first leader of the Soviet Union.
12. **Ferdinand Marcos (The Philippines):** President and Thief of the Filipino people.
13. **Kim Jong-Il (North Korea):** Successor to Kim Il-sung, continued the totalitarian rule in North Korea.
14. **Muammar Gaddafi (Libya):** Longtime ruler of Libya, known for his authoritarian rule.
15. **Robert Mugabe (Zimbabwe):** Longtime ruler of Zimbabwe, whose rule was marked by corruption and economic collapse.
16. **Bashar al-Assad (Syria):** Current president of Syria, whose regime is responsible for widespread human rights abuses in the Syrian Civil War.
17. **Omar al-Bashir (Sudan):** Former president of Sudan, indicted by the International Criminal Court for genocide.
18. **Teodoro Obiang Nguema Mbasogo (Equatorial Guinea):** Longest serving president in the world, known for extreme levels of corruption and human right violations.
19. **Alexander Lukashenko (Belarus):** President of Belarus, known for authoritarian rule and suppression of dissent.
20. **Vladimir Putin (Russia):** Current leader of Russia, continuing the nation's totalitarian rule.

Adolf Hitler: The Art School Dropout Who Redecorated Europe (and Not in a Good Way)

Adolf Hitler, a name synonymous with unfathomable cruelty, was a man of... let's say, *ambitious* artistic aspirations. Before the swastika became a symbol of terror, it was a symbol of his failed artistic career. Imagine, if you will, a world where Adolf found success with watercolours. Europe would have been spared a world war, and the art world would have been subjected to... well, let's not speculate.

His early life was a tapestry of mediocrity and resentment. Born in Austria, he moved to Vienna, the artistic capital of the era, hoping to make his mark. But the Vienna Academy of Fine Arts, with its discerning eye, saw something the world would soon learn: a man incapable of creating beauty, but with a terrifying talent for destruction.

Undeterred, he turned to politics, a stage where his theatrical flair and talent for demagoguery could flourish. His speeches, a mix of nationalist fervour, conspiracy theories, and outright lies, resonated with a disillusioned German populace. He promised a return to glory, a restoration of national pride, and a scapegoat for their woes. And they, in their desperation, believed him.

His rise to power was a masterclass in manipulation. He exploited the weaknesses of the Weimar Republic, played on the fears of the people, and used propaganda to create a cult of personality. He was a master of the "Big Lie," repeating falsehoods until they became accepted as truth. He understood the power of symbols, from the swastika to the goose-stepping parades, creating a sense of order and strength in a chaotic world.

Once in power, he wasted no time in implementing his twisted vision. He established a totalitarian state, suppressing dissent, and persecuting minorities. His obsession with racial purity led to the Holocaust, the systematic extermination of millions of Jews and other "undesirables." It was an industrial-scale operation of evil, a testament to the depths of human depravity.

His foreign policy was equally destructive. He violated treaties, annexed territories, and plunged the world into World War II. He dreamed of a thousand-year Reich, a German empire that would dominate Europe. But his hubris and megalomania led to his downfall. He underestimated the resilience of his enemies and the determination of the Allied forces.

His final act was a pathetic display of self-pity and delusion. Trapped in his bunker, as the Red Army closed in, he blamed everyone but himself for the catastrophe he had unleashed. He took his own life, leaving behind a legacy of death and destruction that continues to haunt the world.

And yet, despite the overwhelming evidence of his evil, there are still those who admire him, who see him as a strong leader, a victim of circumstance. They cling to the myth of the noble warrior, ignoring the reality of the genocidal maniac. It's a testament to the power of propaganda, and the enduring appeal of evil.

Joseph Stalin: The Man Who Managed to Make Russia Even Colder

Joseph Stalin, the "Man of Steel," was a master of political intrigue, a ruthless dictator who transformed the Soviet Union into a totalitarian state. His name evokes images of purges, famines, and the Gulag, a system of terror that claimed millions of lives.

His early life was marked by hardship and violence. Born in Georgia, he was the son of a shoemaker, a man known for his brutality. Stalin's own personality was shaped by this harsh environment, a mix of cunning, paranoia, and a thirst for power.

He rose through the ranks of the Bolshevik Party, proving himself a loyal and ruthless follower of Lenin. He was a master of bureaucratic manoeuvring, consolidating his power and eliminating his rivals. After Lenin's death, he outmanoeuvred his rivals, including Leon Trotsky, and seized control of the Soviet Union.

His rule was marked by a series of brutal policies aimed at transforming the Soviet Union into a communist superpower. He collectivized agriculture, forcing peasants into collective farms, and seizing their land and livestock. This led to widespread famine, particularly in Ukraine, where millions starved to death.

He launched the Great Purge, a campaign of terror that targeted anyone perceived as a threat to his power. Millions were arrested, tortured, and executed, including members of the Communist Party, military officers, and intellectuals. He created a climate of fear and suspicion, where no one was safe.

The Gulag system, a network of forced labour camps, became a symbol of his regime. Millions were sent to these camps, where they endured harsh conditions and brutal treatment. It was a system of mass incarceration, designed to break the spirit of the people.

He was a master of propaganda, controlling the media and rewriting history to suit his narrative. He created a cult of personality, portraying himself as a wise and benevolent leader. He used fear and intimidation to maintain his grip on power, creating a society where dissent was impossible.

His foreign policy was marked by expansionism and aggression. He annexed the Baltic states, invaded Poland, and established communist regimes in Eastern Europe. He played a key role in the Cold War, a conflict that divided the world for decades.

His legacy is one of immense suffering and destruction. He turned the Soviet Union into a police state, where millions lived in fear. He stifled creativity and innovation, creating a society that was both oppressive and stagnant. And yet, there are still those who admire him, who see him as a strong leader, a defender of communism. They ignore the reality of his brutality, clinging to the myth of the benevolent dictator.

Mao Zedong: The Great Leap Forward... Off a Cliff

Mao Zedong, the "Great Helmsman," was a revolutionary leader who transformed China into a communist state. His name evokes images of the Cultural Revolution, the Great Leap Forward, and the Little Red Book, symbols of his radical and often disastrous policies.

His early life was marked by poverty and rebellion. Born into a peasant family, he witnessed the injustices of the old China, the exploitation of the poor by the wealthy landowners. He became a revolutionary, joining the Communist Party and fighting against the Nationalist government.

He led the Long March, a gruelling retreat that solidified his leadership and transformed the Communist Party into a disciplined fighting force. He defeated the Nationalists in the Chinese Civil War, establishing the People's Republic of China in 1949.

His rule was marked by a series of radical policies aimed at transforming China into a communist utopia. He launched the Great Leap Forward, a campaign to rapidly industrialise China and collectivize agriculture. It was a catastrophic failure, leading to widespread famine and the deaths of millions.

He launched the Cultural Revolution, a campaign to purge China of "bourgeois" elements and revive revolutionary fervour. It was a period of chaos and violence, where young people were encouraged to denounce their teachers, parents, and anyone deemed a threat to the revolution.

He was a master of propaganda, using the media to create a cult of personality. He portrayed himself as a wise and benevolent leader, a saviour of the Chinese people. He used the Little Red Book, a collection of his quotes, to indoctrinate the masses.

His foreign policy was marked by isolationism and revolutionary zeal. He supported communist movements around the world, but also isolated China from the West. He engaged in border conflicts with the Soviet Union, highlighting the divisions within the communist world.

His legacy is one of immense suffering and upheaval. He turned China into a totalitarian state, where millions lived in fear. He stifled creativity and innovation, creating a society that was both oppressive and stagnant. And yet, there are still those who admire him, who see him as a revolutionary hero, a liberator of the Chinese people. They ignore the reality of his brutality, clinging to the myth of the benevolent dictator.

Pol Pot: The Farmer Who Sowed Death and Destruction

Pol Pot, the architect of the Cambodian genocide, was a man of chilling ideology and ruthless execution. His name evokes images of the Killing Fields, the forced evacuation of cities, and the systematic extermination of millions.

His early life was marked by a privileged upbringing. Born into a relatively wealthy family, he received a good education, even studying in France. But his experiences in France radicalized him, turning him into a fervent communist.

He returned to Cambodia and joined the Khmer Rouge, a communist guerrilla movement fighting against the government. He rose through the ranks, becoming the leader of the Khmer Rouge and plotting to seize power.

He launched the Cambodian genocide, a campaign to create an agrarian utopia by eliminating anyone deemed a threat to his vision. He emptied the cities, forcing people to work in the fields, and abolished money, religion, and private property.

He targeted intellectuals, ethnic minorities, and anyone perceived as a threat to his regime. He established a system of torture and execution, where millions were killed. The Killing Fields, mass graves filled with the bodies of his victims, became a symbol of his brutality.

He was a master of manipulation, using propaganda to indoctrinate the masses and justify his actions. He created a climate of fear and suspicion, where no one was safe. He turned children against their parents, encouraging them to denounce anyone who disagreed with the regime.

His foreign policy was marked by isolationism and paranoia. He cut off Cambodia from the rest of the world, fearing foreign influence. He engaged in border conflicts with Vietnam, eventually leading to his downfall.

His legacy is one of utter devastation. But it seems today Cambodia is finally climbing out of its doldrums, just mind the dodgy ethanol-laced cocktails and human-slave-run scam farms when you visit.

Alright, let's dive into the fascinatingly tragic world of Benito Mussolini, the Italian strongman who, for a time, convinced a nation he was bringing back the glory of Rome, while mostly just bringing back bad haircuts and worse ideas.

Kim Il-sung: Founder of Kim's North Korea

Kim Il-sung, the founding father of North Korea, is a man who turned a country into a family business and a personality cult into an art form. If there were an award for "Most Over-the-Top Dictator," Kim would have won it posthumously, because even in death, he's still the star of the show. His legacy is a bizarre mix of propaganda, paranoia, and sheer absurdity, making him one of history's most fascinating—and terrifying—figures. Let's take a sarcastic journey through the life and times of everyone's favourite "Eternal President."

Kim Il-sung came to power in 1948, back when the world was still recovering from World War II and the idea of splitting Korea in two seemed like a great plan. Spoiler alert: it wasn't. Kim became the leader of North Korea, and the rest is history—or rather, a never-ending saga of propaganda, oppression, and really bad haircuts. His pitch to the North Korean people? "Hey, things are bad now, but don't worry—I'll make them worse!" And boy, did he deliver.

One of Kim's first moves was to establish a personality cult so intense that it makes Elvis fans look like casual admirers. He declared himself the "Great Leader," because apparently, "Pretty Good Leader" wasn't impressive enough. His image was everywhere—on posters, in schools, even on the sides of mountains. It's like he thought he was a rock star, except the only concert was a never-ending performance of "Bow Down to Me."

Kim's rule was marked by a level of control that would make even Big Brother jealous. He implemented a policy of *Juche*, or self-reliance, which is North Korea's way of saying, "We don't need anyone else, even if it means starving to death." The economy was centralised, dissent was crushed, and the people were told to worship Kim like a god. It's like living in a country-sized cult, except the leader has a really bad sense of fashion.

But Kim wasn't just a brutal dictator; he was also a master of propaganda. His life story was rewritten to make him sound like a superhero, complete with tales of fighting off Japanese invaders single-handedly and inventing rice that could grow in the snow. It's like watching a bad action movie, except the hero is a dictator, and the special effects are just really bad Photoshop.

And then there's his foreign policy, which can best be described as "chaotic evil." Kim started the Korean War in 1950, because apparently, peace was too boring. The war ended in a stalemate, but not before millions of people had died and the Korean Peninsula had been turned into a geopolitical powder keg. It's like starting a fight at a family reunion and then refusing to apologise because you think you're right.

Despite his many, many flaws, Kim had a knack for self-promotion. He loved giving speeches, where he would spout nonsense with a straight face, like a used car salesman trying to sell a lemon. He once claimed he could control the weather, because apparently, he thought he was part wizard. It's like watching a bad magician perform tricks that no one believes, but everyone's too scared to call him out on.

Kim's personal life was just as bizarre as his political career. He had multiple wives and countless children, because apparently, one family wasn't enough to contain his ego. He was also a fan of grandiose gestures, like building massive statues of himself, or holding military parades that looked like a bad Broadway show. It's like he thought he was the star of his own reality show, except the ratings were measured in body counts.

In 1994, Kim Il-sung finally died, but his legacy lives on—literally. He was declared the "Eternal President," because apparently, even death can't stop a dictator's ego. His son, Kim Jong-Il, took over, followed by his grandson, Kim Jong-un, turning North Korea into a family business. It's like a bad soap opera, except the plot is oppression, and the characters are all named Kim.

In conclusion, Kim Il-sung is a cautionary tale about what happens when you give a man too much power and too little sense. He turned North Korea into a nightmare and himself into a caricature of a dictator. So, here's to you, Kim Il-sung. May your legacy be a reminder of the dangers of unchecked power, and may your statues live on as a testament to the absurdity of your reign. And may your family business come to a close, like *asap*.

> Why did the dictator bring a ladder to the bar?
> Because he heard the drinks were on the house!

Benito Mussolini: The Opera Singer Who Forgot the Lyrics (to Democracy)

Benito Mussolini, or "Il Duce" (The Leader), was a master of theatricality. He understood the power of spectacle, the allure of a strongman, and the irresistible charm of a well-tailored uniform. He was, in essence, a political rockstar, though his hits were less "Bohemian Rhapsody" and more "Bohemian Rhapso-*dead*."

Before he was strutting around in military garb, Mussolini was, believe it or not, a socialist journalist and even, briefly, a schoolteacher. He was a fiery orator, a man with a gift for words, though those words often veered into the realm of bombastic nationalism. He was expelled from the Socialist Party for advocating Italian intervention in World War I, a move that foreshadowed his dramatic shift to the far right. It was like a band member suddenly deciding to ditch the acoustic guitar for a full-on heavy metal drum kit.

He formed the Fascist movement in 1919, a ragtag group of disgruntled war veterans and nationalistic zealots. They adopted the fasces, an ancient Roman symbol of power, and a black shirt as their uniform, instantly making them the most stylishly intimidating street gang in Italy. They were the original influencers, setting trends that would soon sweep across Europe, though, admittedly, not in a good way.

Mussolini's rise to power was a masterclass in exploiting chaos. Italy was reeling from the aftermath of World War I, plagued by economic instability and political turmoil. He promised order, stability, and a return to the grandeur of the Roman Empire, a promise that resonated with a population desperate for a strong leader. He was the ultimate hype man, convincing Italians that he was the only one who could "Make Italy Great Again," a slogan with an unfortunately timeless appeal.

The March on Rome in 1922 was a stroke of genius. While the actual march was more of a leisurely stroll than a full-blown military operation, the threat of force was enough to intimidate the King, who appointed Mussolini Prime Minister. It was a political coup disguised as a parade, a theatrical display of power that solidified his control.

Once in power, Mussolini wasted no time in dismantling democracy. He suppressed dissent, banned opposition parties, and established a totalitarian state. He controlled the media, using propaganda to create a cult of personality, portraying himself as a wise and benevolent leader. He was the original "fake news" purveyor, rewriting history and manipulating public opinion to maintain his grip on power.

He embarked on a series of ambitious, and often disastrous, foreign policy ventures. He invaded Ethiopia, a brutal campaign that showcased his imperial ambitions and disregard for international law. He aligned himself with Hitler, a fateful decision that would ultimately lead to Italy's downfall. He was like a small-time gangster trying to buddy up with the head of the mafia, only to find himself dragged into a war he couldn't win.

His economic policies, aimed at creating a self-sufficient Italy, were largely ineffective. He launched the "Battle for Grain," a campaign to increase agricultural production, which resulted in soil depletion and environmental damage. He was like a gardener who thought he could grow crops by yelling at them, ignoring the basic principles of agriculture.

His social policies, aimed at promoting traditional family values and increasing the birth rate, were equally misguided. He encouraged women to stay at home and have babies, while simultaneously promoting a macho image of Italian manhood. He was like a confused parent trying to enforce contradictory rules, creating a society that was both stifling and hypocritical.

His downfall was as dramatic as his rise. As the tide of World War II turned against the Axis powers, Mussolini's grip on power weakened. He was eventually deposed and arrested, only to be briefly rescued by German forces. His final act was a pathetic attempt to establish a puppet state, a desperate grasp for relevance in a world that had moved on.

His execution by Italian partisans in 1945 marked the end of an era. He left behind a legacy of authoritarianism, violence, and ultimately, failure. He was a cautionary tale, a reminder of the dangers of unchecked power and the allure of false promises. He was the opera singer who forgot the lyrics, the strongman who turned out to be weak, the leader who led his nation astray. And yet, even today, there are those who romanticise his rule, who see him as a symbol of national pride. It's a testament to the enduring power of propaganda, and the human capacity for self-deception.

Idi Amin: Ego by numbers

Ah, Idi Amin, the man who turned Uganda into his personal circus and somehow managed to make clowns look like statesmen. If there were an award for "Most Outrageous Dictator," Amin would have won it every year of his reign—and probably demanded a bigger trophy each time. His rule was a chaotic blend of brutality, buffoonery, and sheer absurdity, making him one of history's most infamous strongmen. Let's take a sarcastic stroll through the life and times of everyone's favourite self-proclaimed "Conqueror of the British Empire."

Idi Amin came to power in 1971 through a military coup, because apparently, waiting for an election was too mainstream. He ousted President Milton Obote with the kind of enthusiasm usually reserved for winning the lottery. His pitch to the Ugandan people? "Hey, things are bad now, but don't worry—I'll make them worse!" And boy, did he deliver.

One of Amin's first moves was to declare himself President for Life, because nothing says "humble public servant" like giving yourself a title that sounds like it belongs in a dystopian novel. He also awarded himself a slew of other titles, including "Lord of All the Beasts of the Earth and Fishes of the Seas," which is either the coolest or most ridiculous job title in history, depending on your perspective. It's like he looked at a list of royal titles and thought, "Why not all of them?"

Amin's rule was marked by a level of brutality that would make even the most hardened dictator blush. He purged his enemies—real and imagined—with the kind of efficiency usually reserved for spring cleaning. Estimates of the death toll during his reign range from

100,000 to 500,000, but who's counting, right? It's not like they were people or anything. Just numbers. Amin's approach to governance was simple: if you're not with me, you're against me, and if you're against me, you're dead. It's like a twisted version of "Survivor," except the only prize is not getting killed.

But Amin wasn't just a brutal dictator; he was also a master of the absurd. He once declared economic war on Israel and then asked them for help building his military. He expelled Uganda's Asian population, seizing their businesses and handing them over to his cronies, which promptly crashed the economy. It's like watching someone set their own house on fire and then blame the neighbours for the smoke.

And then there's his foreign policy, which can best be described as "chaotic neutral." Amin loved to pick fights with other countries, but only if they were too far away to actually do anything about it. He once threatened to invade Israel, which is like a toddler threatening to arm-wrestle a bodybuilder. He also declared himself the "Conqueror of the British Empire," which is impressive considering he never actually conquered anything. It's like claiming you've climbed Mount Everest because you once walked up a hill.

Amin's personal life was just as bizarre as his political career. He had multiple wives and countless children, because apparently, one family wasn't enough to contain his ego. He was also a fan of grandiose gestures, like parading around in a white suit and hat, or driving around Kampala in a convertible while waving to crowds like he was in a parade. It's like he thought he was the star of his own reality show, except the ratings were measured in body counts.

Despite his many, many flaws, Amin had a knack for self-promotion. He loved giving interviews, where he would spout nonsense with a straight face, like a used car salesman trying to sell a lemon. He once claimed he could live underwater for 30 minutes, because apparently, he thought he was part fish. It's like watching a bad magician perform tricks that no one believes, but everyone's too scared to call him out on.

In 1979, Amin's reign of terror finally came to an end when Tanzanian forces and Ugandan exiles invaded Uganda and ousted him. He fled to Libya, then Iraq, and finally Saudi Arabia, where he lived out his days in exile. It's like the universe decided it had had enough of his nonsense and sent him to time-out.

In conclusion, Idi Amin is a cautionary tale about what happens when you give a man too much power and too little sense. He turned Uganda into a nightmare and himself into a caricature of a dictator.

Speaking of caricature, let's delve into the chilling narrative of Augusto Pinochet, the Chilean general who traded his uniform for a dictator's mantle, leaving a legacy of deep division and human rights violations.

Augusto Pinochet: The General Who Traded Democracy for a Dictatorship (and a Lot of Sunglasses)

Augusto Pinochet was a career military man, a general who rose through the ranks with a reputation for loyalty and discipline. Little did Chile know that this seemingly unassuming figure would orchestrate one of the most brutal dictatorships in Latin American history. He was, in essence, a wolf in sheep's clothing, or perhaps, a general in a suit of iron.

His rise to power was a calculated manoeuvre, a coup d'état that shattered Chile's long-standing democratic tradition. In 1973, amidst growing political polarization and economic turmoil, Pinochet, with the backing of the military, overthrew the democratically elected socialist president, Salvador Allende. It was a violent takeover, marked by the bombing of the presidential palace and Allende's tragic death.

Pinochet justified his coup by claiming he was saving Chile from communism, a narrative that resonated with some sectors of society, particularly the upper class and those fearful of social upheaval. He was the self-proclaimed saviour, the strongman who would restore order and stability. But his definition of order was chillingly authoritarian.

Once in power, Pinochet established a military junta, a regime that ruthlessly suppressed dissent and crushed opposition. He dissolved Congress, banned political parties, and silenced the media. He was the ultimate censor, deciding what Chileans could see, hear, and speak.

His regime was notorious for its systematic human rights violations. Thousands of people were arrested, tortured, and disappeared. The infamous Villa Grimaldi, a torture centre in Santiago, became a symbol of his brutality. He was the architect of terror, creating a climate of fear that permeated Chilean society.

His economic policies, implemented by a group of economists known as the "Chicago Boys," were a radical experiment in neoliberalism. He privatized state-owned enterprises, deregulated markets, and cut social spending. While these policies led to some economic growth, they also exacerbated inequality and left many Chileans struggling. He was the economic surgeon who performed radical procedures, with mixed results.

His foreign policy was marked by close ties with the United States, particularly during the Cold War. He was seen as a staunch anti-communist ally, receiving support from the US government despite his human rights record. He was the Cold War warrior, fighting a battle against communism, even if it meant sacrificing democracy.

His rule was characterised by a cult of personality. He cultivated an image of a strong and decisive leader, often seen wearing sunglasses and military attire. He was the fashion-forward dictator, projecting an image of power and control.

His downfall came in 1988, when he held a plebiscite to extend his rule. To his surprise, the Chilean people voted "no," rejecting his dictatorship and paving the way for a return to democracy. It was a stunning rebuke, a testament to the resilience of the human spirit.

Even after stepping down as president, Pinochet remained a powerful figure, serving as senator for life. However, his past caught up with him. He faced numerous legal challenges, both in Chile and abroad, related to human rights abuses. He was the aging dictator, facing the consequences of his actions.

His legacy is deeply divisive. For some, he is remembered as a strong leader who saved Chile from communism. For others, he is a brutal dictator who committed heinous crimes. He was, and remains, a figure of intense controversy, a symbol of the dark side of power. He left a nation with deep wounds, still healing, and still debating his role in Chilean history.

Okay, let's venture into the opulent, yet terrifying, world of Saddam Hussein, the Iraqi strongman who fancied himself a modern-day Nebuchadnezzar, but mostly just ended up with a lot of bad statues and a really big hole in the ground.

Saddam Hussein: The Man Who Loved Statues (Almost as Much as He Loved Himself)

Saddam Hussein, a name that conjures up images of desert palaces, grandiose statues, and a healthy dose of paranoia, was a master of self-promotion. He saw himself as a modern-day Saladin, a champion of the Arab world, though his actions often painted a far less flattering picture. He was, in essence, a dictator with a flair for the dramatic, a leader who confused absolute power with absolute style.

His early life was a mix of poverty and ambition. Born in a village near Tikrit, he joined the Ba'ath Party, a pan-Arab socialist movement, and quickly rose through the ranks. He participated in a failed assassination attempt on the Iraqi Prime Minister, earning himself a stint in prison and a reputation for ruthlessness. He was the aspiring revolutionary, learning the ropes of political violence.

He seized power in 1979, becoming the President of Iraq and establishing a totalitarian regime. He consolidated his control through violence and intimidation, eliminating his rivals and creating a climate of fear. He was the ultimate boss, brooking no dissent and demanding absolute loyalty.

His rule was marked by a series of wars and conflicts. He launched a brutal war against Iran, a conflict that lasted for eight years and resulted in immense casualties on both sides. He was the warrior king, leading his nation into a bloody and ultimately futile conflict.

He invaded Kuwait in 1990, a move that triggered the First Gulf War and led to his eventual downfall. He miscalculated the international response, underestimating the resolve of the United States and its allies. He was the gambler who bet it all and lost.

His regime was notorious for its human rights abuses. He used chemical weapons against his own people, particularly the Kurds, in a campaign of genocide. He tortured and executed political opponents, silencing dissent and creating a climate of terror. He was the tyrant, ruling through fear and violence.

He built numerous palaces and monuments to himself, showcasing his wealth and power. He commissioned grandiose statues of himself, portraying himself as a heroic figure. He was the narcissist, obsessed with his own image and legacy.

He cultivated a cult of personality, controlling the media and portraying himself as a wise and benevolent leader. He used propaganda to manipulate public opinion and maintain his grip on power. He was the spin doctor, crafting a narrative that masked his brutality.

His downfall came in 2003, when the United States and its allies invaded Iraq, overthrowing his regime. He was captured, put on trial, and eventually executed. He was the fallen dictator, brought to justice for his crimes.

His legacy is one of violence, oppression, and ultimately, failure. He left behind a nation scarred by war and conflict, a society traumatised by his brutality. He was a cautionary tale, a reminder of the dangers of unchecked power and the destructive consequences of megalomania. He was the man who loved statues, but ultimately, his own legacy crumbled like sand.

Okay, let's journey into the sepia-toned world of Francisco Franco, the Spanish general who traded democracy for a very long nap (for the country, that is), a fondness for parades, and a profound belief that he was doing Spain a massive favour.

Francisco Franco: The General Who Thought Spain Needed a Really, Really Long Siesta (from Democracy)

Francisco Franco, or "El Caudillo" (The Leader), was a master of... well, let's call it "strategic ambiguity." He was a man of few words, but those words often carried the weight of absolute power. He was, in essence, the strong, silent type, if the strong, silent type also happened to be a dictator.

His early life was a classic tale of military ambition. He rose through the ranks of the Spanish army, serving in Morocco and earning a reputation for bravery and... let's say, a certain lack of progressive ideals. He was the career soldier, dedicated to the military, and perhaps a little too dedicated to the old ways.

The Spanish Civil War (1936-1939) was his moment. He led the Nationalist forces, backed by Nazi Germany and Fascist Italy, against the Republican government. It was a brutal and devastating conflict, tearing Spain apart and leaving a legacy of deep divisions. He was the wartime leader, fighting for what he believed was the soul of Spain, though his methods were anything but soulful.

His victory in the Civil War ushered in a long and repressive dictatorship. He established a totalitarian regime, suppressing dissent, banning opposition parties, and silencing the media. He was the ultimate gatekeeper, controlling what Spaniards could read, watch, and even think.

His regime was notorious for its human rights abuses. Thousands of people were executed or imprisoned for their political beliefs. The infamous Valle de los Caídos (Valley of the Fallen), a monumental complex built by forced labour, became a symbol of his power and his cruelty. He was the iron fist, crushing any opposition with ruthless efficiency.

His economic policies were a mix of autarky (self-sufficiency) and protectionism. He aimed to make Spain independent from foreign powers, but his policies often resulted in economic stagnation and hardship. He was the economic isolationist, trying to build a wall around Spain, both literally and figuratively.

His social policies were deeply conservative and traditionalist. He promoted Catholicism as the state religion, suppressed regional cultures and languages, and enforced strict moral codes. He was the social conservative, trying to turn back the clock to a mythical golden age.

He cultivated a cult of personality, portraying himself as a divinely appointed leader. He used propaganda to create an image of a wise and benevolent ruler, a father figure to the Spanish people. He was the benevolent dictator, or at least, he wanted people to think he was.

His foreign policy was marked by neutrality during World War II, a decision that allowed him to survive the conflict. He maintained close ties with the United States during the Cold War, receiving economic and military aid in exchange for his anti-communist stance. He was the

Cold War survivor, navigating the treacherous waters of international politics.

His death in 1975 marked the end of an era. He left behind a Spain that was deeply divided but also poised for a transition to democracy. He was the last of the great European dictators, a relic of a bygone age.

His legacy is complex and controversial. For some, he is remembered as a strong leader who brought stability to Spain after a period of chaos. For others, he is a brutal dictator who committed heinous crimes. He was, and remains, a figure of intense debate, a symbol of the enduring power of the past. He was the general who thought Spain needed a long siesta, but ultimately, it was Spain that woke up and moved on.

Alright, let's take a wild ride into the extravagant and often bizarre world of Muammar Gaddafi, the Libyan leader who fancied himself a philosopher-king, but mostly just ended up being a very eccentric and heavily armed tourist.

Muammar Gaddafi: The Philosopher-King Who Packed a Golden Gun (and a Tent)

Muammar Gaddafi, or "Brother Leader," was a master of contradictions. He was a revolutionary who became a dictator, a pan-Africanist who meddled in other nations' affairs, and a man who preached simple living while living in opulent tents and surrounded by female bodyguards. He was, in essence, a walking paradox, a leader who defied easy categorisation.

His early life was marked by humble beginnings. Born into a Bedouin family in the desert, he was inspired by Egyptian President Gamal Abdel Nasser's pan-Arab nationalism. He joined the military and led a bloodless coup in 1969, overthrowing the monarchy and establishing the Libyan Arab Republic. He was the young revolutionary, seizing power with a mix of charisma and military might.

He introduced his own political philosophy, the "Third International Theory," outlined in his "Green Book." It was a mishmash of socialism, Arab nationalism, and Islamic principles, a unique blend that he claimed was a superior alternative to capitalism and communism. He was the philosopher-king, writing his own rulebook and expecting the world to follow along.

His rule was marked by a mix of social welfare programs and authoritarianism. He used Libya's oil wealth to fund infrastructure projects, healthcare, and education, improving the lives of many Libyans. However, he also suppressed dissent, banned political parties, and controlled the media. He was the benevolent dictator, providing for his people while denying them basic freedoms.

His foreign policy was erratic and often destabilising. He supported various revolutionary movements and terrorist groups around the world, earning him a reputation as a rogue state sponsor. He was the international meddler, funding and arming various factions, often with disastrous consequences.

He was known for his flamboyant style and eccentric behaviour. He travelled with an entourage of female bodyguards, lived in a Bedouin tent, and wore elaborate military uniforms. He was the eccentric leader, a spectacle to behold, both at home and abroad.

His regime was notorious for its human rights abuses. He tortured and executed political opponents, silenced dissent, and created a climate of fear. The Abu Salim prison massacre, where hundreds of inmates were killed, became a symbol of his brutality. He was the ruthless dictator, willing to use violence to maintain his grip on power.

His downfall came during the Arab Spring in 2011. Protests against his rule erupted, and a civil war ensued. NATO intervention helped the rebels overthrow his regime. He was captured and killed by rebel forces, ending his 42-year rule.

His legacy is complex and controversial. For some, he is remembered as a nationalist leader who brought stability and prosperity to Libya. For others, he is a brutal dictator who committed heinous crimes. He was, and remains, a figure of intense debate, a symbol of the contradictions and complexities of post-colonial leadership. He was the philosopher-king who packed a golden gun, a leader who left behind a nation in chaos.

Alright, let's delve into the tragic saga of Robert Mugabe, the Zimbabwean liberation hero who morphed into a ruthless autocrat, leaving a once-promising nation in economic ruin and political turmoil.

Robert Mugabe: The Liberation Hero Who Forgot the Script (and Wrote a Really Bad Sequel)

Robert Mugabe was a complex figure, a man who began as a beacon of hope and ended as a symbol of oppression. He was a liberation fighter, a skilled orator, and a shrewd political operator, but also a man consumed by power and paranoia. He was, in essence, a tragic hero who fell from grace, a leader who lost his way.

His early life was marked by intellectual pursuits and political activism. He was educated at prestigious universities, including Fort Hare in South Africa and the University of London. He became involved in the Zimbabwean liberation struggle, fighting against white minority rule. He was the educated revolutionary, driven by a desire for justice and equality.

He played a key role in the Lancaster House Agreement, which led to Zimbabwe's independence in 1980. He was hailed as a hero, a symbol of national unity and reconciliation. He was the liberator, the man who brought freedom to Zimbabwe.

His early years as Prime Minister were marked by progress and stability. He invested in education and healthcare, improving the lives of many Zimbabweans. He was the nation builder, laying the foundation for a prosperous future.

However, his rule gradually became more authoritarian. He consolidated his power, suppressed dissent, and eliminated his rivals. He was the power consolidator, unwilling to share power with anyone.

His land reform program, aimed at redistributing land from white farmers to black Zimbabweans, was a catastrophic failure. It was implemented violently and chaotically, leading to economic collapse and food shortages. He was the land grabber, destroying the country's agricultural base.

His regime was notorious for its human rights abuses. He used violence and intimidation to silence his opponents. He rigged elections, manipulated the media, and created a climate of fear. He was the tyrant, ruling through fear and violence.

He presided over a period of hyperinflation, economic collapse, and widespread poverty. Zimbabwe became a pariah state, isolated from the international community. He was the economic destroyer, ruining the nation's economy.

He clung to power for decades, refusing to relinquish control even as his health deteriorated. He was the stubborn ruler, unwilling to let go of power.

His downfall came in 2017, when he was ousted in a military coup. He was forced to resign, ending his 37-year rule. He was the deposed leader, finally removed from power.

His legacy is deeply divisive. For some, he is remembered as a liberation hero who fought for Zimbabwe's independence. For others, he is a brutal dictator who ruined the country. He was, and remains, a figure of intense controversy, a symbol of the dangers of unchecked power and the tragic consequences of a leader's descent into tyranny. He was the liberation hero who forgot the script, a leader who turned his back on the very people he once fought to liberate. His family (and stolen riches) live on in his self-declared home of Singapore, where he spent most of his final days being loved by the Singaporean people.

Okay, let's plunge into the world of Vladimir Lenin, the Russian revolutionary who swapped the Tsar's crown for a worker's cap (and a whole lot of red flags), leaving a legacy that's still debated with the fervour of a Trotsky vs. Stalin argument.

Vladimir Lenin: The Lawyer Who Traded Briefs for Bombs (and a Really Big Beard)

Vladimir Ilyich Ulyanov, better known as Lenin, was a man of intense conviction, a revolutionary who believed in the inevitable triumph of communism with the zeal of a door-to-door salesman pushing the latest miracle cure. He was, in essence, a political evangelist, spreading the gospel of Marx with the fervour of a convert.

His early life was marked by tragedy and radicalization. His brother was executed for plotting to assassinate the Tsar, a pivotal event that fuelled Lenin's revolutionary fervour. He was the vengeful brother, channelling his grief into a lifelong commitment to overthrowing the Tsarist regime.

He became a lawyer, but his true passion was politics. He joined the revolutionary movement, becoming a leading figure in the Bolshevik faction of the Russian Social Democratic Labour Party. He was the intellectual revolutionary, using his sharp mind and persuasive rhetoric to advance his cause.

He spent years in exile, honing his revolutionary theories and building a network of supporters. He was the exiled leader, plotting his return to Russia and the overthrow of the Tsar.

The chaos of World War I provided the opportunity he had been waiting for. The Tsarist regime was crumbling, and Lenin seized the moment, returning to Russia and leading the Bolsheviks to power in the October Revolution of 1917. He was the revolutionary leader, seizing power in a moment of crisis.

His rule was marked by radical changes and brutal repression. He nationalized industry, collectivised agriculture, and withdrew Russia from World War I. He established a one-party state, suppressing dissent and creating a climate of fear. He was the radical reformer, transforming Russia into a communist state, but at a great cost.

He established the Cheka, a secret police force that used terror and violence to eliminate his opponents. He was the ruthless dictator, willing to use any means necessary to maintain his grip on power.

He was a master of propaganda, using the media to create a cult of personality. He portrayed himself as a wise and benevolent leader, a saviour of the Russian people. He was the spin doctor, crafting a narrative that masked his brutality.

His legacy is complex and controversial. For some, he is a revolutionary hero, the founder of the Soviet Union and a champion of the working class. For others, he is a ruthless dictator who established a totalitarian regime and paved the way for Stalin's horrors. He was, and remains, a figure of intense debate, a symbol of the enduring power of ideology and the tragic consequences of revolutionary violence. He was the lawyer who traded briefs for bombs, a leader who changed the course of history, but left a legacy stained with blood.

Let's now explore the era of Ferdinand Marcos, the Philippine president who started with promises of progress and ended with a legacy of corruption, martial law, and a shoe collection that could rival a small museum.

Ferdinand Marcos: The War Hero Who Became a Kleptocrat (and Owned More Shoes Than Imelda)

Ferdinand Marcos was a master of political theatre, a charismatic leader who initially captured the hearts of the Filipino people. He was a war hero (or so he claimed), a brilliant orator, and a shrewd political strategist. But beneath the surface of his charm and charisma lay a hunger for power and wealth that would ultimately lead to his downfall.

His early life was a blend of academic achievement and political ambition. He was a brilliant student, a skilled lawyer, and a decorated war hero (though the veracity of some of his war stories has been questioned). He was the rising star, the man destined for greatness.

He rose through the ranks of Philippine politics, becoming a senator and eventually president in 1965. He promised a "New Society," a vision of progress and prosperity for the Philippines. He was the reformer, the man who would lead the Philippines to a brighter future.

However, his rule gradually became more authoritarian. He used the threat of communist insurgency and civil unrest to justify his increasingly repressive policies. He was the fearmonger, using the spectre of instability to consolidate his power.

In 1972, he declared martial law, suspending civil liberties and establishing a dictatorship. He justified this move by claiming it was necessary to save the country from chaos. He was the strongman, seizing absolute power in the name of national security.

His regime was notorious for its human rights abuses. Thousands of people were arrested, tortured, and killed for their political beliefs. He silenced the media, suppressed dissent, and created a climate of fear. He was the tyrant, ruling through fear and violence.

His economic policies were marked by corruption and cronyism. He and his cronies plundered the nation's wealth, enriching themselves while the majority of Filipinos lived in poverty. He was the kleptocrat, using his power to amass a fortune.

His wife, Imelda Marcos, became a symbol of extravagance and excess. Her vast collection of shoes, jewellery, and artwork became a symbol of the regime's corruption. She was the first lady of excess, living a life of luxury while her countrymen struggled.

He cultivated a cult of personality, portraying himself as a wise and benevolent leader. He used propaganda to manipulate public opinion and maintain his grip on power. He was the spin doctor, crafting a narrative that masked his corruption and brutality.

His downfall came in 1986, when a popular uprising, known as the People Power Revolution, forced him to flee the country. He was ousted from power, ending his 20-year rule. He was the deposed dictator, forced into exile.

His legacy is deeply divisive. For some, he is remembered as a strong leader who brought stability to the Philippines. For others, he is a corrupt dictator who ruined the country and stole billions from its people. He was, and remains, a figure of intense controversy, a symbol of the dangers of unchecked power and the corrosive effects of corruption. He was the war hero who became a kleptocrat, a leader who betrayed the trust of his people. Today his son carries on his name and Presidency, much like the many so-called democracies in Southeast Asia.

Bashar al-Assad: the Ophthalmologist Who Tried to Blind the World

Ah, Bashar al-Assad, the ophthalmologist-turned-dictator who somehow managed to turn Syria into a real-life game of *Civilization*—except instead of building wonders, he's been busy building rubble. If there were an award for "Most Likely to Survive a Decade of Chaos," Assad would win it hands down. This guy has clung to power with the tenacity of a barnacle on the hull of a sinking ship, and somehow, against all odds, he's still here. Let's dive into the tragicomedy that is Bashar al-Assad's reign.

First, let's set the stage. Bashar wasn't even supposed to be the guy. He was the backup son, the understudy thrust into the spotlight after his older brother, Basil, died in a car crash in 1994. Bashar was living the quiet life in London, studying to be an eye doctor, when suddenly he was called back to Syria to take over the family business—dictatorship. Imagine going from prescribing glasses to presiding over a regime infamous for its brutality. Talk about a career change!

When Bashar took over in 2000 after his father, Hafez al-Assad, died, there was a brief moment of hope. People called it the "Damascus Spring." Bashar was young, Western-educated, and seemed like he might bring some reforms. Spoiler alert: he didn't. The "Damascus Spring" turned into the "Damascus Deep Freeze" faster than you can say "authoritarian crackdown." Bashar proved that the apple doesn't fall far from the tree—or in this case, the iron fist doesn't fall far from the dictatorship.

Then came the Arab Spring in 2011, and Syria was not immune. Protests broke out, demanding freedom and democracy. Bashar's response? A masterclass in how *not* to handle dissent. Instead of listening to his people, he decided to crush them with the subtlety of a sledgehammer. Peaceful protests were met with bullets, tanks, and torture. The situation escalated into a full-blown civil war, and Bashar's strategy seemed to be: "If you can't win the hearts and minds, just bomb them into submission."

And bomb he did. Bashar's regime, with help from his buddies in Russia and Iran, turned Syria into a wasteland. Cities like Aleppo and Homs, once bustling centres of culture and history, were reduced to rubble. Millions of Syrians fled the country, creating one of the worst refugee crises in modern history. But hey, at least Bashar got to keep his throne, right? Priorities!

Let's not forget Bashar's charming habit of using chemical weapons on his own people. Sarin gas, chlorine bombs—you name it, he's probably used it. It's like he looked at the Geneva Conventions and thought, "Cool story, bro," before tossing them in the trash. The international community has condemned him repeatedly, but Bashar just shrugs it off like it's a bad Yelp review. Sanctions? War crimes accusations? Pfft. He's got Russia and China blocking anything meaningful at the UN, so he's basically untouchable.

And then there's the propaganda. Bashar's regime has a knack for spinning even the most horrific events into something vaguely positive. Hospitals bombed? "Terrorist hideouts destroyed." Civilians killed? "Collateral damage in the fight against extremism." It's like watching a used car salesman try to sell a lemon as a luxury vehicle. The sheer audacity is almost impressive.

Through it all, Bashar has managed to maintain an eerie calmness. He gives interviews where he denies everything, blames everyone else, and acts like he's the victim in all this. It's like watching a kid with chocolate all over his face insist he didn't eat the cake. The man has the poker face of a champion, even as his country burns around him.

In the end, Bashar al-Assad is a tragic figure—not because of any personal suffering, but because of the suffering he's inflicted on millions of Syrians. He's a dictator who turned a country into a cautionary tale, a man who chose power over peace at every turn. And yet, somehow, he's still standing (last heard he has now "relocated" to Moscow, near his buddy-bro V-Putin). Whether that's a testament to his ruthlessness or the world's failure to stop him is up for debate. But one thing's for sure: Bashar al-Assad is a reminder that sometimes, reality is stranger—and darker—than fiction.

Omar al-Bashir: Outstayer of Welcome, at Home and Abroad

Omar al-Bashir, the man who ruled Sudan for 30 years with the subtlety of a bull in a china shop, is a figure so controversial that even his moustache seems to be plotting something. If there were a "How to Stay in Power Forever (While Making Everyone Hate You)" guide, Bashir would have written the foreword. His reign was a masterclass in how to turn a country into a geopolitical dumpster fire while somehow managing to dodge accountability like a ninja in a room full of laser beams. Let's take a sarcastic stroll through the life and times of everyone's favourite Sudanese strongman.

Bashir came to power in 1989 through a military coup, because apparently, waiting for an election was too mainstream. He ousted the democratically elected government with the kind of enthusiasm usually reserved for Black Friday sales. His pitch to the Sudanese people? "Hey, things are bad now, but don't worry—I'll make them worse!" And boy, did he deliver.

One of Bashir's first moves was to implement Sharia law, because nothing says "progress" like rolling back human rights to the 7th century. Women, minorities, and anyone who enjoyed things like "freedom" or "basic dignity" were suddenly out of luck. But hey, at least Bashir got to feel like a medieval caliph, which was clearly his lifelong dream.

Then there's the small matter of Darfur. In the early 2000s, Bashir decided that the best way to deal with a rebellion in the region was to unleash the Janjaweed, a militia so brutal they make pirates look like boy scouts. The result? A genocide that left hundreds of thousands dead and millions displaced. Bashir's response? A shrug and a "Who, me?" that would make even the most seasoned politician blush. The International Criminal Court (ICC) eventually indicted him for war crimes, crimes against humanity, and genocide, making him the first sitting head of state to be charged with such crimes. But Bashir, ever the optimist, treated the indictment like a parking ticket—annoying, but not exactly life-ruining.

Despite being an international pariah, Bashir had a knack for playing the victim. He loved to complain about how the West was out to get him, as if the ICC charges were just a big misunderstanding. "Oh, you think I committed genocide? No, no, that was just a really intense game of tag gone wrong." His ability to dodge accountability was almost impressive. He travelled to other countries, attended Arab League summits, and generally acted like a man who hadn't been accused of orchestrating one of the worst humanitarian crises of the 21st century.

But Bashir wasn't just a war criminal; he was also an economic wizard. Under his "leadership," Sudan's economy went from bad to "are we still using money or just bartering goats now?" He squandered the country's oil wealth, mismanaged resources, and turned Sudan into one of the poorest nations on Earth. Inflation was so high that people needed wheelbarrows full of cash to buy a loaf of bread. But hey, at least Bashir had a nice palace to live in. Priorities, right?

Bashir's downfall finally came in 2019, when the Sudanese people decided they'd had enough of his nonsense. After months of protests, the military ousted him in a coup. The man who had ruled with an iron fist for three decades was suddenly out of a job. It was a rare moment of poetic justice, like watching a villain in a movie finally get their comeuppance. But even in defeat, Bashir managed to be infuriating. He was placed under house arrest, which, for a guy accused of genocide, is basically a slap on the wrist. Meanwhile, the Sudanese people were left to pick up the pieces of the mess he'd made.

In the end, Omar al-Bashir is a cautionary tale about what happens when power goes unchecked for too long. He's a reminder that dictators may rise, but they always fall—eventually. And while his reign was a disaster for Sudan, it did give us one thing: a textbook example of how *not* to run a country. So, here's to you, Omar al-Bashir. May your legacy be a warning to future generations, and may your moustache forever haunt your mugshot.

Teodoro Obiang Nguema Mbasogo: the Record (and People) Breaker

Teodoro Obiang Nguema Mbasogo, the man, the myth, the legend—well, at least in his own mind. If there were an Olympic event for holding onto power, Obiang would be the undisputed gold medallist, having ruled Equatorial Guinea since 1979 with the kind of iron grip that would make a boa constrictor jealous. He's the kind of leader who makes you wonder if he's ever heard the phrase "term limits" or if he just assumes it's something you order at a restaurant.

Obiang's rise to power is the stuff of political satire. He overthrew his uncle, Francisco Macías Nguema, who was, by all accounts, a real piece of work. Macías was so paranoid and brutal that he made Stalin look like Skippy. So, when Obiang took over, the people of Equatorial Guinea probably thought, "Well, it can't get worse than this, right?" Spoiler alert: it didn't get much better. Obiang may have ditched his uncle's penchant for public executions, but he kept the family tradition of authoritarianism alive and well.

Under Obiang's "leadership," Equatorial Guinea has become a textbook example of the resource curse. The country is swimming in oil money, but you'd never know it by looking at the living conditions of most of its citizens. While Obiang and his family live in opulent luxury—think private jets, mansions, and enough yachts to start a small navy—the average Equatorial Guinean is lucky if they have access to clean water. It's like winning the lottery and then watching your neighbour spend all the money on gold-plated toilet seats while you're stuck with an outhouse.

Obiang's political strategy is as subtle as a sledgehammer. He wins elections with percentages that would make even the most brazen dictator blush. We're talking 95% of the vote, folks. At that point, why even bother with the charade of an election? Just declare yourself "Supreme Eternal Leader" and be done with it. But no, Obiang insists on going through the motions, as if anyone actually believes the results. It's like a magician pulling a rabbit out of a hat, except the rabbit is stuffed, and the hat is rigged with explosives.

And let's not forget Obiang's commitment to "democracy." He's the kind of guy who gives speeches about the importance of freedom and human rights while his government jails journalists, suppresses dissent, and generally treats the constitution like a suggestion rather than a rulebook. It's like a chef who preaches about healthy eating while secretly deep-frying everything in sight.

But perhaps the most impressive thing about Obiang is his ability to stay in power for over four decades. In a world where leaders come and go faster than TikTok trends, Obiang is the political equivalent of a cockroach—resilient, hard to kill, and always lurking in the shadows. He's survived coup attempts, international criticism, and even a bizarre incident where he claimed to have divine protection. That's right, Obiang once said that God was on his side, which raises the question: what kind of deity looks at a corrupt, authoritarian regime and thinks, "Yeah, that's my guy"?

In conclusion, Teodoro Obiang Nguema Mbasogo is a living testament to the absurdity of power. He's a leader who has managed to turn a resource-rich country into a kleptocratic playground, all while maintaining a straight face. Love him or hate him (and let's be honest, it's probably the latter), you have to admit: the man knows how to keep a job. If nothing else, Obiang serves as a cautionary tale about what happens when one person has too much power for too long. And if that doesn't make you laugh, well, maybe you're just not cynical enough.

Alexander Lukashenko: Keeping the Soviet Dream Alive

Alexander Lukashenko, the self-proclaimed "last dictator in Europe," is a man who has turned Belarus into his personal fiefdom with the finesse of a Soviet-era bureaucrat who never got the memo that the Cold War ended. If there were an award for "Most Likely to Pretend It's Still 1985," Lukashenko would win it every year. His reign has been a masterclass in how to cling to power while making your country the laughingstock of the continent. Let's dive into the absurdity that is Lukashenko's Belarus.

Lukashenko came to power in 1994, back when dial-up internet was still a thing, and he's been clinging to his position ever since with the tenacity of a limpet on a rock. He's the political equivalent of that one guest at a party who doesn't realise it's time to leave. His initial pitch to the Belarusian people was that he'd bring stability and prosperity. Fast forward nearly three decades, and the only thing he's brought is a never-ending supply of cringe-worthy moments and human rights abuses.

One of Lukashenko's favourite hobbies is pretending Belarus is still part of the Soviet Union. He's kept Soviet-style collective farms, state-controlled media, and a secret police force that would make the KGB proud. It's like he's running a historical reenactment, except the participants didn't sign up, and the script is a tragedy. His nostalgia for the USSR is so strong that you half expect him to show up to meetings in a Lenin costume, waving a hammer and sickle.

Then there's his approach to democracy, which can best be described as "democracy-ish." Elections in Belarus are about as free and fair as a game of Monopoly where one player owns all the properties and makes up the rules as they go along. Lukashenko wins every election with Soviet-level percentages—we're talking 80%, 90%, sometimes even more. At this point, he might as well just declare himself "Supreme Eternal Leader" and save everyone the trouble of pretending to vote.

Lukashenko's response to dissent is about as subtle as a sledgehammer. Protests? Crack them down. Opposition leaders? Jail them. Independent media? Shut them down. His go-to move is to blame everything on "foreign interference," as if the Belarusian people are incapable of wanting change without some shadowy Western puppet master pulling the strings. It's like watching a bad spy movie where the villain's plan is so ridiculous that you can't help but laugh.

And let's not forget Lukashenko's unique approach to public relations. This is a man who once suggested that playing ice hockey and working on a farm could cure COVID-19. Yes, you read that correctly. While the rest of the world was scrambling to develop vaccines and implement lockdowns, Lukashenko was out there telling people to hit the rink and milk some cows. It's like he's living in an alternate universe where science is optional, and common sense is a foreign concept.

Despite his many, many flaws, Lukashenko has somehow managed to stay in power. Part of this is due to his ability to play both sides of the geopolitical game. He's cozy with Russia when it suits him, but he's not above flirting with the West if it means getting a better deal. It's like watching a bad rom-com where the protagonist can't decide between two love interests, except instead of love, it's about maintaining a stranglehold on power.

In 2020, Lukashenko's grip on power was seriously challenged for the first time. Mass protests erupted after yet another rigged election, and for a moment, it looked like the Belarusian people might finally be rid of him. But Lukashenko, ever the survivor, cracked down hard, with help from his buddy Vladimir Putin. The protests were brutally suppressed, opposition leaders were jailed or forced into exile, and Lukashenko emerged—once again—as the "winner."

In conclusion, Alexander Lukashenko is a living relic of a bygone era, a man who has turned Belarus into his personal playground while the rest of the world looks on in disbelief. He's a reminder that sometimes, reality is stranger—and sadder—than fiction. And speaking of bygone eras, here's someone from the glory days of Soviet KGB-dom and for whom the methods of eliminating the opposition with dastardly devices is very much alive...

Vladimir Putin: Keeping Imperial Russia alive, Soviet Style

Ah, Vladimir Putin, the man, the myth, the meme. If there were an Olympic event for political machinations, Putin would be the reigning champion, with a gold medal in "How to Stay in Power Forever" and a silver in "Making the World Nervous." He's the kind of leader who makes you wonder if he's a Bond villain, a KGB throwback, or just a really committed history buff who thinks the Cold War was the good old days. Let's take a sarcastic journey through the life and times of everyone's favourite strongman.

Putin came to power in 1999, back when the world was worried about Y2K and boy bands ruled the airwaves. He was appointed Prime Minister by Boris Yeltsin, who apparently thought, "Hey, this guy looks trustworthy." Spoiler alert: he wasn't. Putin quickly moved up to President, and the rest is history—or rather, a never-ending saga of power grabs, propaganda, and perplexing shirtless photo ops.

One of Putin's first moves was to consolidate power, because apparently, sharing is for kindergarteners. He centralized authority, muzzled the media, and turned Russia into a managed democracy—which is like a democracy, except without the pesky parts like free elections and civil liberties. It's like calling a dictatorship a "participatory autocracy." Sure, you can participate, but don't expect your vote to count for much.

Then there's Putin's approach to opposition, which can best be described as "creative." Critics, journalists, and political rivals have a habit of meeting unfortunate ends—poisonings, mysterious falls from windows, and the occasional polonium tea. It's like a real-life game of Clue, except the answer is always "Putin in the Kremlin with the nerve agent." The man has turned political assassination into an art form, and while the international community raises eyebrows, Putin just shrugs and says, "What can I say? Accidents happen."

Putin's foreign policy is equally subtle. He's the guy who looks at a map and thinks, "You know what this needs? More Russia." His annexation of Crimea in 2014 was a masterstroke of geopolitical trolling, leaving the world wondering if they should be outraged or impressed. And let's not forget his adventures in Syria, where he turned a civil war into a showcase for Russian military might. It's like he's playing Risk, except the board is the real world, and the stakes are human lives.

But Putin isn't just a political mastermind; he's also a man of the people. By "the people," of course, I mean his inner circle of oligarchs, who have grown fabulously wealthy while the average Russian struggles to make ends meet. It's like a reverse Robin Hood—steal from the poor, give to the rich, and call it economic policy. Meanwhile, Putin's propaganda machine churns out stories of his heroic exploits, from wrestling tigers to discovering ancient Greek artifacts. It's like a superhero origin story, except the superpower is shameless self-promotion.

And then there's the cult of personality. Putin is everywhere in Russia—on TV, in schools, even on t-shirts. He's portrayed as a strong, decisive leader who can do no wrong. It's like living in a country-sized fan club, except dissent is not allowed, and the membership fees are your freedom. His approval ratings are always sky-high, which is what happens when you control the media and jail anyone who disagrees with you.

Despite all this, Putin has a knack for playing the victim on the world stage. He loves to complain about NATO expansion, Western sanctions, and how everyone is out to get poor, innocent Russia. It's like watching a schoolyard bully cry foul because someone took his lunch money. The man has a talent for turning his aggression into a sob story, and somehow, there are always people willing to buy it.

In conclusion, Vladimir Putin is a fascinating figure—a blend of cunning, ruthlessness, and sheer audacity. He's turned Russia into his personal playground, all while keeping the world on edge. Whether you love him or hate him (and let's be honest, it's probably the latter), you have to admit: the man knows how to play the game. So, here's to you, Vladimir Putin. May your reign be as short as your patience for democracy, and may your legacy be a cautionary tale for future generations. And maybe, just maybe, consider retiring to a nice dacha somewhere. And take your cronies with you.

> What do you call a dictator's vacation?

> A state of emergency*—because he can't relax unless everyone else is panicking.

Appendix: Dictator Hall of Fame

Welcome to the Dictator Hall of Fame, where we celebrate the larger-than-life personalities who set the gold standard (sometimes literally) for authoritarian excellence. These titans of tyranny not only crushed opposition but also turned ruling into an art form – sometimes with a lot of sequins, questionable statues, and the occasional shoe addiction. And because every dictator needs a partner in crime (or at least someone to clap for them while wearing pearls), we're including their equally dazzling spouses.

Without further ado, here are the awards you never knew these infamous leaders deserved. Please, hold your applause... unless it's mandatory.

1. Best Dressed Dictator

Winner: Muammar Gaddafi

Nobody worked Bedouin chic quite like Gaddafi. With his flowing robes, sunglasses-game so sharp they could cut glass, and enough gold embellishments to rival a Eurovision stage, this Libyan leader ensured every coup d'état looked fabulous. His wardrobe whispered, "I have oil money, and I dare you to question it."

Honourable Mention for Spouse Style Power goes to **Madame Nhu**, the so-called "First Lady of South Vietnam." She turned parliament debates into catwalks with her glamorous áo dài redesigns and fiery rhetoric. Who says fashion and politics don't mix?

2. Most Creative Propaganda

Winner: Joseph Stalin

Few could match Stalin's ability to turn airbrushing photographs into a national sport. Rivals disappeared not just from the Kremlin but from all historical archives, as though they were merely figments of the collective imagination. His masterpiece? Rebranding totalitarian terror as a "Five-Year Plan for Progress." Bravo!

Honourable Mention goes to **Eva Perón**, who gave propaganda a Broadway twist in Argentina. Mixing glamor, charity events, and political ambition, she made populism look like a Vogue spread. Is it manipulation if it comes with a sparkly ball gown? Absolutely, but we're still clapping.

3. Biggest Misuse of Public Funds

Winner: Ferdinand and Imelda Marcos

This power duo from the Philippines redefined extravagant spending. Ferdinand preferred country-sized Swiss bank accounts, while Imelda's true love was her shoe collection—featuring over 3,000 pairs. They both inspired one clear takeaway for aspiring dictators everywhere: Why fix potholes when you can shop Ferragamo?

Pro Tip: If you can't justify the spending, call it "cultural preservation," as Imelda did with her cavernous closet. Genius.

4. Most Over-the-Top Personality Cult

Winner: Kim Jong-Il

Forget modesty—Kim Jong-Il's cult of personality featured supernatural births (complete with double rainbows), personal bests in golf (a hole-in-one EVERY time, obviously), and claims of controlling the weather with his mood. Who wouldn't worship a man capable of pulling off such celestial multitasking?

Honourable Mention to **Jiang Qing**, wife of Chairman Mao, who played diva-director for China's Cultural Revolution propaganda operas. Think less "dictator's spouse" and more "unhinged artistic director with unlimited budget and zero critics alive to complain."

5. Most Family Drama in a Regime

Winner: Kim Jong-un

Do siblings count as opposition? Kim Jong-un thinks so! His mysterious treatment of relatives recalls Thanksgiving dinners gone horribly, horribly wrong. Don't even ask what his retirement holiday card list looks like—you're probably on it, and not in a good way.

Honourable Mention goes to **Catherine de' Medici**, technically not a "dictator," but who deserves her own Netflix series for the amount of scheming and poisoning she tolerated at family dinners.

6. Most Lawless Love Story

Winner: Benito Mussolini and Rachele Mussolini

Italy's fascist pride, Benito, elevated romantic chaos to an Olympic sport, maintaining multiple mistresses, while Rachele Mussolini, his wife, somehow pretended she didn't notice. Talk about "standing by your man" even when he's essentially writing a soap opera starring himself.

Honourable Mention for unshakable loyalty goes to **Svetlana Alliluyeva**, Stalin's wife, who walked into the reigning paranoia-bear-pit of Soviet politics and STILL thought, "This seems romantic."

7. Most Unhinged "Royal" Spending

Winner: King Louis XVI and Marie Antoinette

Okay, technically absolute monarchs, but we're sneaking the OG "eat cake" power couple into the Hall of Fame because no one disrespected bread-making peasants with grander panache. Marie's allegedly-blurted love for pastry sealed her fate and taught future dictators one timeless truth—don't anger people who fix snacks.

Pro Tip for Dictators: Learn from the French Revolution. If you're going big with Versailles-style parties, make sure everyone can still afford basic carbs.

8. Weirdest Influence on Pop Culture

Winner: Saddam Hussein

Saddam's career wasn't short on weird behaviour, but his bizarre obsession with writing romance novels lands him this coveted spot. Who else could helm a regime of terror while penning Harlequin-esque literature where heroes suspiciously resembled...himself? Stay multi-talented, kids.

Honourable Mention goes to **Evita Perón** again, who inspired an Andrew Lloyd Webber musical. If you don't leave behind at least one show-stopping number, did you even rule gloriously?

9. Best "It's Not Me, It's the Spies" Award

Winner: Nicolae Ceaușescu

The Romanian dictator blamed every power outage, empty grocery store, and revolution brewing in his backyard on shady foreign spies. It was the ultimate "it's not me, it's them" relationship excuse—except with 23 million people. Even his wife, **Elena Ceaușescu**, stood by him, insisting their suffering nation just didn't appreciate their *magnificent scientific brilliance*.

Pro Tip for Aspiring Dictators: A scapegoat works wonders until said scapegoat overthrows you. Careful there.

10. Most Passive-Aggressive Use of Architecture

Winner: Saddam Hussein

Nothing says "I'm the boss" quite like rebuilding Babylon... but for yourself. Saddam ensured his name was etched on every brick, you know, just to remind folks who was "restoring history." If reincarnated, Nebuchadnezzar would probably sue.

Special Mention to **Leila Ben Ali**, wife of Tunisia's Zine El Abidine, who allegedly built a massive private zoo on palace grounds... because ruling is stressful, and somewhere, a giraffe *is required*.

11. Fiercest Hair Game

Winner: Saparmurat Niyazov (Turkmen Bashi)

Not technically for his hair (which was basic dictator-issue), but for banning everyone else's bad dye jobs. The Turkmen dictator outlawed hair and beards that didn't meet his standards—ensuring no shaggy rebellion on *his* watch. Flamboyant? Absolutely. Tyrannical? Without question.

Honourable Mention to **Eva Braun**, Adolf Hitler's longtime partner, for perfect curls in bunker conditions. Spin-off idea: *Dictators' Spouses Face Extreme Makeovers*.

12. Biggest Fan of Naming Things After Themselves

Winner: Mobutu Sese Seko

The Zairian president's ego reached *calamitous* heights when he renamed cities, rivers, and even children in his own honour. Fun fact: his full title was 17 words long, with "the all-powerful warrior" wedged in there for flavour.

Honourable Mention to **Grace Mugabe**, who allegedly had Zimbabweans refer to her simply as *Mother of the Nation*. No word if she handed out stern curfews alongside those vibes.

13. Best Reality-Denying "Economic Plan"

Winner: Hugo Chávez

Chávez's economic strategies for Venezuela earned him top marks for optimism, with inflation soaring faster than his social media meme-worthy speeches. His "Bolivarian socialism" promises paired with empty shelves proved that running a country isn't just about slogans.

Special Shoutout to his successor Nicolás Maduro who kept the trend alive.

14. Best Use of Statues to Say, "I'm Watching You"

Winner: Enver Hoxha

The Albanian dictator blanketed his small country with so many concrete bunkers, heads of Marxist leaders, and his own likeness that even paranoid ants couldn't sneak by unnoticed. "Big Brother" vibes scored *en masse*.

Honourable Mention to **Ferdinand Marcos**, whose grave was basically a shrine of "unretired" power long after his literal demise. Imelda would approve.

15. Most Misleading Nickname

Winner: Francisco Franco ("El Caudillo the Benevolent")

Generalissimo Franco's *self-granted* nickname did everything except reflect benevolence. It's like calling a 3-hour dentist appointment "fun." Subtle shade, Franco... very subtle.

Honourable Mention to **Anne-Marie Southey**, Napoleon III's mistress, allegedly nicknamed "the sweet dove" first, later followed with titles rephrased by unhappy wives everywhere.

16. Best Paranoia-Induced Reforms

Winner: Idi Amin

From banning multi-coloured pens (a.k.a. "tools of conspiracy") to mandatory nighttime curfews *for owls,* Idi Amin practically invented creating personal rules like Jenga towers. Who knew paranoia could reshape nature?

Special Mention for **his many wives**, one of whom allegedly returned her ceremonial gifts because the wedding was a surprise! Spoiler alert? Disturbing understatements galore.

17. Most Dramatic Posthumous Reveal

Winner: Hideki Tojo

The Japanese Prime Minister during World War II, Tojo, maintained a calm and collected demeanour while orchestrating some of the most devastating military campaigns. Posthumously, his role in atrocities and war crimes came to light, making him a prime example of how history loves to unmask the "polite villain."

Honourable Mention to **Magda Goebbels**, wife of Joseph Goebbels, whose dramatic end in Hitler's bunker cemented her as a symbol of blind loyalty to a doomed regime. If there were an award for "Most Over-the-Top Exit," she'd win hands down.

Final Hall of Fame Takeaway

Behind every great dictator (or wannabe) is a trail of propaganda, dubious awards, stolen artwork, and questionable fashion choices. Whether they ruled with terror, charm, or absurdity, they knew one thing for sure – history loves a good spectacle. And if you can make your reign unforgettable, the **Dictator Hall of Fame** will be here waiting to amplify your dubious achievements.

Remember, future Hall-of-Famers, greatness isn't just about power. It's about the shoes, the shades, the headlines, and the memes that will last probably forever.

Author's Note

I wrote this as a means of poking fun at the absurdities of authoritarian behaviour, but it's important to remember the real-world consequences of such regimes. Humour can be a way to critique power, but it's always good to approach sensitive topics with care. In this collection, my motive is to revisit history and remind readers of the kind of figures in our collective memory who have shaped our lives in more unfortunate ways than one. The idea is to mock them and belittle their combined legacies and to drive home the truth that autocracies often lead to corruption and ultimately offer little benefit to anyone but themselves and their cronies. Disastrously for us, we still find people who are inspired to be the next Hitler or Idi Amin or Pol Pot. Hopefully with this book, we are reminded as to why these despots fail and why we should never *ever* allow them to return.

H. M. Tan

www.ingramcontent.com/pod-product-compliance
Lightning Source LLC
Chambersburg PA
CBHW070503100426
42743CB00010B/1740